LOVE
Heals All Wounds

D1344940

LOVE
Heals All Wounds

A Roadmap from Fear
to Unlimited Possibilities

LINDA F. KENT

Published by Clearly Rising, LLC

Clearly Rising LLC

Published by Clearly Rising, LLC

ISBN (paperback): 979-8-218-33701-8
ISBN (ebook): 979-8-218-33702-5

Book design and production by www.AuthorSuccess.com

Printed in the United States of America

I give my deepest gratitude to the spiritual teachers
I have experienced whether in person or in books that have
elevated me by offering new thought that enriched my life.
You have been the true pioneers of a new age of enlightenment.
I am carrying the torch for you.

Contents

"Love is within us.
It cannot be destroyed.
It can be ignored.
To the extent that we
abandon love, we will
feel it has abandoned us.
Denying love is our only
problem, and embracing
it is the only answer.
Through the power of love,
we can let go of past
history and begin again.
Love heals, forgives
and makes whole."

ERNEST HOLMES
THE SCIENCE OF MIND

Foreword

We live in a world where fear is rampant. Daily, the news and other media reinforce the belief that we are victims of outside forces beyond our control. In deep self-protection, many people isolate themselves from life or escape into distractions and addictions. Humanity is issuing a massive call for help.

When a book comes along that can alleviate fear and soothe our psychic wounds, it deserves attention, study, and application. Linda Kent has achieved just such a noble goal. Through her honest sharing of her own journey from fear to love, from dysfunction to health, from pain to wellness, she provides a map for us to heal our own lives.

Of richest importance, Linda identifies healing as a process that unfolds from the inside out. It is tempting to focus on symptoms without unveiling their cause. Yet a holistic vision of life recognizes that mind and spirit are the source of our physical and emotional experience. Behind all manifestation is belief. When we pierce the source of our pain, we can heal it effectively and permanently.

As Linda so effectively explains, love is the great healer. Fear is based on illusion, and love is founded in truth. This book contains many pertinent examples, from the author's life and others' lives, that make transformation so much more than just an idea. When we apply universal truth to Earthly challenges, healing happens naturally and organically.

This book affirms your power to source your own life in co-creation with God. Linda masterfully underscores how, just as we have used our Earthly mind to conjure our issues, we can apply our divine mind to offset them. She offers numerous spiritual practices to stay connected to Source. We need these like oxygen for our souls. Here you will find many tips to align with yourself and the universe. The chapters are neatly laid out with lots of tools and summaries. You will feel relieved to have this handy guide at your fingertips.

Every crossroads we face calls us to choose between love and fear. Relationships, finances, career, and health form templates upon which we learn and grow. *Love Heals All Wounds* embraces all of these facets as opportunities to choose peace. Every encounter, event, and experience are brilliantly designed to serve our awakening, if we are willing to use it as such. If you find yourself at such a crossroads, guidance is available to you. Just as the author has been brilliantly directed, so are you.

You are holding a well-thought-out roadmap to help you make successful transitions in relationships, career, and from the physical to the spiritual. As life has gotten faster and change happens more quickly, navigating transitions becomes a paramount skill. Today, in one lifetime many people go through numerous relationships or marriages, different jobs and careers, and for some, lots of living situations. We have all agreed to accelerated learning. Without a spiritual foundation, change can be scary. A spiritual framework of life embraces all change as a blessing. Looking at life and change through the lens of love and appreciation makes all the difference.

We teach more through our example than our words. Linda Kent is unashamedly open about her life, which gives us entrée to masterfully extract wisdom from our own experiences. I have a great deal of respect for this woman who has learned to make life work on her behalf, and now assists you to do the same. We have all felt wounded, and we all crave love. May the words and ideas you find in the pages that follow bring you the peace your heart deeply seeks.

–Alan Cohen

Inspirational Author of thirty-one books, including best-seller *A Course in Miracles Made Easy* and award-winning *A Deep Breath of Life*, keynote speaker, and contributing writer for the number one best-selling series *Chicken Soup for the Soul*.

Introduction

We either grow beyond our fears or we become victims of the fear. Most of us, during various times in our lives, become entrapped in a web of fear that creates barriers and holds us back from what we might dream or hope to achieve. We bury our emotional wounds deep within our inner being to hide it from the world. We go through life experiencing heartache and watch our opinion of ourselves slowly diminish. We begin to exist, not expecting too much from life and hoping that we can keep a roof over our heads, pay the bills, and sometimes find a little escape every once in a while. Have you ever felt this way?

At one time, my life was just like this, living many years merely existing because I believed "this is how life is." At the time, there was no one to guide me because everyone else I knew was experiencing the same kind of life. This eventually led me to check out of life once in my early twenties, not by trying to commit suicide or escape by using drugs, but by making a decision. I decided that I could not live in a world where there was so much deceit and fear. I said to myself, "If this is the way the world is meant to be lived, I do not want any part of it."

I felt myself slowly fading away. I called my husband to come home. I could no longer take care of our two small children. That was when I went catatonic. I can't explain how I did this, but I was certain that the world I had been living in was not supporting me to stay. The hospital admitted me and a psychiatrist was consulted. As a result, I received seven shock treatments. What the shock treatments achieved was wiping out my fears as well as my memories. I gradually came back, but with a total shift in my personality and character. The journey of my recovery was discovering what I would accept in my life and what could not enter. This different person that I felt I had become was like a new personality living within me. I was so shy and timid before, and now, my personality was very direct and expressive of what I felt. Sometimes I was too abrupt, and I realized that I needed to find a balance when I saw people's reactions to what I would say. This is a more drastic, but true, example of how fear can overtake your life.

As years passed, I worked very hard to remember my past. I wanted to understand and heal the past that I had lived and to see this world from a different perspective. My journey took me forty years of discovering the depth of love and why the existence of fear is present. The experiences with deaths of loved ones gave me insight into the spiritual world after we leave Earth. The most important thing I learned through ten years with my spiritual teacher, Carla Gordan, is the value of the inner spirit and the gifts that unfold as a result of tuning into that spirit.

Love Heals All Wounds will take you on a journey of how I dissected fear to discover and expose its true nature, how love is the healer, that beliefs and awareness can heal the wounds of the heart, and death is really the transformation of life. There is no death, but an extension of what never dies.

This book has been spiritually guided to bring you the truth of what lives inside each person, even though we are uniquely different in what we create. We are all united in spirit and separated by fear. You will experience how the restriction of fear can be paralyzing and can create walls or barriers to keep you from discovering your true nature and capabilities of what you can create to offer life.

The book will bring you awareness of the limitations and barriers that are faced every day in life and how knowledge and growth of increased value, self-worth, and self-love can set you free. This is why we either grow beyond our fears or we become victims of it.

When you are finished reading, you will:

- Know how to manage fear when it confronts you and know how to heal it

- Understand how Love is the healer of all wounds whether mental, emotional, or physical

- Have greater knowledge of the importance of personal growth, self-love, and awareness of life

- Discover the spiritual world that supports all of our hopes, dreams, and fulfillment of what we create

- Realize we are multi-dimensional beings living in a third-dimensional world

- Find that death is not real and have new insights with a higher perspective of life, whether on Earth or in spirit

You are meant to create a masterpiece called your life. It comes from inner growth, transformation through fear, and the discovery of Love that dwells within.

You will find at the end of each chapter a Healing Love Practice that includes The Awareness from that chapter with questions and My Affirmation for your thoughts and reflection. The affirmation can be said aloud as many times as you wish. You may find that journaling your own life experiences can assist you with clarification and insight.

The paragraphs throughout the book *in italics* are spiritually guided messages I received during my writing. We are all intuitive and can receive messages from Spirit to the extent we attune or become receptive to this dimension and open our hearts to receive messages from a loving and supportive spiritual world.

CHAPTER 1

The Pain of Living Without Purpose

Fear breeds when you lack direction in life. The nature of fear is to keep us limited and stop us from seeking the reality of our true nature. The beliefs we develop from fear are limiting as we interact with our daily lives. The belief system we adapt to takes form in what we experience in our lives.

Children's lives vary depending on the environment growing up and whether it is supported with love or fear limitations. Most likely, it is a combination of the two. Parents instill their beliefs into our consciousness believing they are helping to structure our minds. This is great when the beliefs are love-based. Often, fear beliefs are instilled to keep us safe, such as:

"Don't run out into the street! It's dangerous!"

"Don't touch the stove! It's hot and will burn you!"

"Don't talk to strangers!"

Do you remember any of these from your childhood or from what you have taught your own children? The helpful precautions are for our safety, but in truth, are based in fear. Parents see potential danger and the natural instinct is to protect. What happens if we have parents who are negative and always talk about not having enough? What belief does this create? A belief in *lack*, and it will reach out to show us there is never enough to go around. Limitations are the seeds of fear.

As a child, I felt emotionally insecure and uncertain while interacting with other people. I believe this may be true with most introverted children. My sensitivity was strong, and I felt emotions from other people that I did not understand. Love and fear played a definite role with how comfortable I felt. The fearful emotions were difficult and uncomfortable as I felt myself wanting to automatically withdraw. The happy emotions made me more comfortable to come out of my shell and be more open. As a child, I did not feel safe from my insecurities I kept inside, which I did not understand at the time were fear. What I was feeling and experiencing from the adult world was a lack of sensitivity to my fears. There was no one to guide me to help me understand this. I lived out my childhood the best I could, but not under the best circumstances. I stayed quiet as much as I could. My sister was my safe haven, as she accepted and supported me unconditionally with love, and as a result, I followed her direction. My uncertainties and insecurities felt safe with her. My parents lacked the awareness or the knowledge to help. As it turned out, they had problems of their own.

My sensitivity as a child allowed me to feel emotions from other people that were different under the surface than what they projected outwardly. What I mean by that is I could see through what a person wanted the outside world to believe when something contrasted what they were actually feeling. Being introverted had me step back and be the observer of the people around me. I did not know as a child how to use this, nor how valuable it would be for my future. I always wished I could be that outgoing person that could draw people to them. That was not my forte as a child.

My mother and father separated and divorced when I was nine years old. My mother felt the burden of becoming a single mother with four children, and the youngest one born with spina bifida, which made things at home more challenging. My mother was under a lot of pressure in the late 1950s to work and support four children. Divorce was frowned upon back then. This was hard for all of us, as we were in a time of surviving. If things weren't bad enough, my mother began investigating the idea of putting us in foster care. I heard her talk about this, and the fear built within me that made me believe somehow that I was not good enough or loving enough for her to want me to stay. I felt as if it were my fault that she was going to send us away. My insecurities were mounting each day as I felt that somehow God overlooked me. Because I was introverted, it was difficult to express what was going on inside. I could never ask if I was loved or important because I was afraid of the answer. My life reflected that belief back to me.

You can imagine the number of accumulating fears that grew because of situations and circumstances I faced. Do you remember having fears from your own childhood experiences that were not the ideal love-based situations? Fear can grow so easily when you are not conscious or aware of its presence.

Just before the process of foster care was completed, my mother backed out of placing us there. I was nine years old when I was sent to live with my aunt and uncle, who had no children of their own. This separated me from my sisters and brother. The understanding came later as an adult that my aunt was relieving some of the burden on my mother. However, I didn't understand that reality at the time, so I navigated my childhood confused and uncertain as to where my place was in this uncertain world. I settled into living as an only child with my aunt and uncle while missing my family back home.

One day, the phone rang and my uncle answered. Completely out of my nature, I picked up the other phone quietly, only hearing the words that were being told to my uncle. What I heard was that my brother had been hit by a car in front of our home and he was pronounced dead at the hospital. I absorbed the words, but I did not know what to do with it emotionally, so I pretended I did not hear the conversation. This was my way of hiding from what my emotions could not endure. My uncle told my aunt, and they came to my room where I had retreated. They told me the news of my brother's death. I already knew, but I could not tell them because I was afraid. My heart felt this numbness and I did not know how to react. I was confused. I did not know something of this magnitude could happen. I did not want to believe that it was true, but reality told me differently. My emotions felt frozen. I retreated into a void that my heart was not ready to embrace. "This is not real. This is not really happening," I told myself.

We drove to my home, where my family met. My father had arrived and the grief escalated. My next-door neighbor took me outside and separated me from all the sorrow for a bit. We were sitting in her front yard, next door to my house, when an ambulance arrived. They took a gurney inside, and as they came out of the house, my father was laying on it, screaming out the depth of his grief, heartbreak, and the devastation he felt. His only son was gone. I had never witnessed or heard such sounds of deep mourning. What I could feel through my sensitivity from my father was a state of pain of such depth in my own body. I knew his sorrow was coming from the depth of his soul. My neighbor had put her hands over my ears in an attempt to silence what I was hearing, but the sound was piercing. I was devastated because I needed him to be my strength that I did not have. I held my emotions inside me to be strong for him.

The next day we went to the funeral home. As we entered the room, I saw my seven-year-old brother's body lying in a coffin at a distance. I stayed in the back of the room because I was afraid to go closer. The minister was there and saw me. He walked toward me and led me to the coffin. He held his arm around me and made me stay and look at my brother. The barrier that I created to keep me strong began to weaken and I was fighting to hold back the tears. I wanted to get away, but the minister's arm was strong and he held me there. I did not want to see my brother laying in a coffin so lifeless. As I began to feel the reality of his death, the tears began to flow. The barrier of my emotions was breaking down like a dam caving in from water putting so much pressure on it. My emotions came alive and I no longer had control. I felt my body weakening and then everything inside of me had to let go. The minister had to hold me up as my body was collapsing with the surrender of my reality, the loss of my brother. I had tried so hard to prevent the acceptance of the reality that faced me. My brother was not in my life anymore. I never forgot what it took for our family to move through his death.

Many children have grown into adulthood, like you, who have faced similar circumstances where we are challenged by loss, fear, and sorrow. What do we do with all these emotions? We form beliefs around them. That is when fear can claim its greatest victories without you even knowing! We have many choices of how we live with the memories of our loved ones that leave. Circumstances vary immensely. Look back to see, if you can remember, any of the circumstances around a loved one's death, especially if it was an unexpected death, as to what you believed about what happened. It's important that you examine and see if there is anything there that formed a belief and how it impacted your life. What you are looking for is any fear surrounding the outcome of your experience. Fear might look like anger, withdrawal, depression, giving up, or not caring about your life anymore. If you are at peace when you go back to remember, like I am now, then you have neutralized any fear that may have been present.

The awakening and healing I received from my spiritual teacher, Carla Gordan (see more on Carla in chapter 3), as she took me back to this portion of my life when I was ready to receive it, gave me all the ingredients to heal the experience of foster care that I came close to experiencing. I held the portion of almost being put in a foster home and housed it as a deep inner wound. I had not been aware of it whatsoever. When this time was brought to the surface as an adult during one of my sessions, I cried over the fear of being pulled away from my home. I felt my inner child's fear and all the emotion she was experiencing. I had not realized how devastated I was. Once this awareness had surfaced, I followed up by going to my mother and asking her a few weeks later, in a loving way, why she had contemplated placing us in foster care. My mother gave me the answer that allowed the complete healing. She told me that she had a premonition that something bad was going to happen to one of us. She did not know who. My mother continued by saying that she was pursuing this to protect us from the premonition she had. She decided that she could not go through with the foster care. My mind connected the dots and I realized that my brother was hit by a car and died in front of our home about a year after the premonition. That was my healing, knowing that she loved us so much that she was trying to protect us. That changed the perception of what I had buried and brought to the surface to gain the insight and awareness to resolve the perfect healing from the wound I had carried for so many years.

What I have learned in experiencing fear is that there is usually a trigger that brings up a painful wound, sometimes when you least expect it. I have a friend, Sally, who experienced this very thing. A group of us were together in the mountains to reconnect. All was loving and we were all enjoying being together, reuniting after a year apart. One late afternoon, Sally accidentally dropped a glass, which shattered all over the floor. When this accident happened, the group did not apply any meaning other than glass just broke and could be replaced. For Sally, it carried a far deeper meaning than we were aware of at the time. Her emotions changed from surprise at the glass falling and breaking to horror as memories and emotions flooded to the surface of what that meant for her. Someone handing her a broom to clean it up also triggered an inner response that she felt, "I have screwed up!" and the broom represented shame, as she interpreted it. She dropped the broom, devastated by what had happened, and ran to her room crying. Debra, from our group, followed Sally to her room where she shared all the emotions that came up from the past. Eventually, both of them returned and we sat around the table that evening to share our love and support for Sally in her release of her fears.

Sally had a belief from past experiences to fear relationships, as she would have one or two friends come into her life and they would slowly fade away. As an adult, Sally had more than one experience that supported this belief. Her husband left her abruptly, and then her best friend left her in the same manner a year later, ending their relationship. The love from what Sally thought were her closest allies transformed into fear of not knowing when sudden, unexpected betrayal would come from her loving relationships. She carried these emotional wounds within, not trusting love in any intimate or loving relationships.

Sally felt the love that everyone had for her. What devastated her was that she thought she had just destroyed that love with us by breaking the glass, and it would be like her past experiences. Instead, we embraced her with love so powerful that the fear she had lived with from her past could not survive. We did not go away, but we stayed, loved, and supported her. This was the most beautiful awakening moment, not only for Sally, but for all of us. Love and connection are so powerful, and when you experience it at this level of healing, the doorway of Love opens and you feel the vibrant qualities of unconditional love flowing through your being. Everyone in our group of nine received it that evening.

Pain without purpose is defined as a fear you have harbored deep within, and when something happens in your life that triggers a response within you and it arises, you will have the love and support surrounding you to recognize it, heal, and find peace. You release the burden of that fear. It no longer has power over you.

Have you experienced something fearful that you buried for years that came to the surface years later to be healed and released?

Healing Love Practice

The Awareness

Love-based beliefs move me forward.

What beliefs have you discovered that are
not supporting your life?

What fears would you heal to elevate your life?

My Affirmation

Love provides the support and courage to
help me heal the fears within.

CHAPTER 2

Love is an Inside Job

If someone stopped you on a street corner and asked, "If you had a choice between love and fear, which would you choose?" of course, most everyone would say love. And yet, we go through each day and there are many situations that we face unexpectedly where we may be caught off guard. Fear is in and out of our lives all day long. We search to find love in our life. This is our natural instinct for those who have searched for a loving relationship: to connect, to love, and to live happily ever after. Some couples meet early in life, marry, have children, and stay married for the remainder of their lives. I have met couples like this throughout my life and wished at times I could have experienced how that felt.

The truth of Love continually searches for rest in the hearts of individuals, couples, families, and even friends. Often, we search for connection to the Love that is our true nature, thinking Love is outside of ourselves. Many have not yet discovered that the Love we so diligently search for is not a boyfriend, a husband, or a friend. The Love we seek resides within, and until we can awaken to this reality, we search for love outside ourselves. We enter relationships and they are filled with the perception of love, but as time goes on, we discover another side of the relationship. The dynamics of compatibility within love and fear, boundaries and limitations come into the picture.

What is it that draws us to another person, sometimes with great results and sometimes with heartbreak? Most of us have heard about the "Law of Attraction." My opinion is that it's the vibrational qualities that attracts someone into your life. The energy or vibration of Love and fear is drawn to you every day. We have an innate nature to pick up on these. I was in and out of many relationships before I discovered the Love I was seeking could not be found in another person.

I was nineteen years old and seeking an existence away from what I had in my past. Still unaware of the belief system inside me that carried a lot of heaviness, I ventured out in a way unusual to my nature. I was totally unaware that I was being driven by fear. I had a boyfriend, Ronnie, whom I had dated all through high school. He was my best friend and the man that I intended to marry when he came back from the Navy. I knew he was leaving soon for basic training, and deep inside, I was terrified about not having him near me. The fear of being alone with my mother was greater than I imagined.

Around the same time, I was the maid of honor in my best friend's wedding. I met the best man at the rehearsal dinner, and he caught my attention immediately. Jim was handsome, outgoing, and personable. He connected easily with people he was meeting for the first time. Jim lived in California and had flown to Dallas for the wedding. The connection we had with each other was mutual. The wedding ceremony and reception were too short-lived from our perspective, and it seemed that we needed more time. We were growing more connected and not wanting the night to end. The end came and I could only take the memories of the connection and elevation I felt as I drifted back into my routine of living at home. Two weeks after the wedding, I received a phone call from Jim. I was so surprised. We talked for a lengthy time and he told me he was flying back to Dallas that weekend. Jim asked if I would be available for dinner while he was here. "Of, course," I said, and I had something exciting to look forward to.

Jim took me to a restaurant that was more upscale than places where I usually ate. I was enjoying the attention that seemed to be drawn to us by his charm with the restaurant staff. We were enjoying each other's company and then it happened. Jim asked me to marry him and go back to Los Angeles. He was seven years older than me. I thought about Ronnie leaving for training and my fear of him not being here. Being alone was a greater fear than accepting Jim's proposal and leaving that weekend.

Taking a step back from this true story, I now ask myself, "Who marries a man after meeting and knowing him for only two weeks?"

That's insane to me now! I married pre-maturely at nineteen, freed from living at home. It was a fear-driven decision to give up my best friend whom I loved and who was going away. It is sad to think now that staying with my mother terrified me more than a high-risk marriage to a man I had only met two weeks prior at a wedding. I was naïve and so young that I did not have any counseling concerning living as an adult. I ad-libbed and followed what was expected of me after agreeing to marry him. Just before we were officially married by a Justice of the Peace, my stomach became upset and I vomited in the bathroom toilet. That was a sign that I reflected on later, telling me I did not know what I was getting into, and yet, something within me did.

My life was fabulous in the beginning. Living in Los Angeles was exciting and my husband drove a fancy car. However, he wanted to tell me what clothes to wear and how to style my hair. Initially, I saw this as his way of helping me to fit in and to be accepted. He showered me with so many experiences that were spectacular to a nineteen-year-old in the entertainment world. My life had been so limited with my family. He was giving me a taste of a world that I had never experienced, and the first three months living in Los Angeles were mouth-dropping moments! He wined and dined me and we went to popular shows with famous singers. I enjoyed our relationship and was very impressed with the life he was introducing me to. There was more fun than I could have possibly imagined.

As I reflect on this time, I thought that getting married would make my fears subside or disappear. There is a distraction period in any new relationship when you are so busy with the newness that the fears within are dormant for a time until life gives a new twist. I had not learned yet about the power of my belief system and fear. I was focused more on what I didn't want than what I wanted. I associated my fear of living with my mother as more painful than moving into the unknown with a new marriage. I learned over time that the fears followed me and would keep building until I reached a point of reckoning.

We had only been in Los Angeles for about six months when I found out my youngest sister was very ill. Days before Christmas, we packed our bags and headed to Texas. I went to see Beth in the hospital. She was in so much pain, but when she heard my voice, a smile grew on her face. That smile was so welcoming and I felt so happy that she was overjoyed that I was there. She was blind, having lost her vision at age four, and used sound as her primary sense and she recognized my voice. They let her come home from the hospital for Christmas Eve, and we had our normal celebration with dinner and a gift exchange. I knew we had made the right decision to be there. Later that evening, Beth returned to the hospital. The next morning, we were notified that she had passed away during the night, peacefully, in her sleep. We later learned, after an autopsy, that her death was caused by a massive calcium deposit on her brain. This was the second loss of a sibling. My heart mourned from her passing. I was grateful, though, that she passed peacefully. After her death, we decided to move back to Dallas and leave Los Angeles behind.

I became pregnant and had a beautiful daughter. Only seventeen months later, I had a baby boy. I was in my early twenties with two small children. Patterns that I became aware of during these next few years made me concerned about the man who I married and thought I knew. I observed that he was always overspending on extravagant things that we could easily live without. He would always put on a show for people to make them believe he was something that he was not. I became uncomfortable with the lies that he could say so convincingly, and that people believed. I began to feel that I was living a lie, without any substance to my life. I no longer wanted the life that I felt I was being forced to live. I had tried to leave him, but he would not let me. I was a housewife and mother who had no car during the day, and I began to feel that I was a prisoner in my own home.

Finally, I had had enough! I was at my breaking point and a catatonic experience that sent me to the hospital was my escape from a life I had no control over. After seven shock treatments, I was very altered in my thinking. My past had been erased and I was attempting to understand and search for who this person was, living in my body.

My life was very fragile and I had no filters. If I thought someone was looking at me wrong, I would not hesitate to tell them what I thought. This was totally out of character for the person I was before the shock treatments. I relied on my sister and mother to help bring back memories of my past. Whether good or bad, I felt empty without the memories. I was very sensitive during my recovery, and I had to control my reactions that were uncomfortable. This was difficult, because there was a harshness within me that I was not accustomed to. Things would come out of my mouth that were uncomfortable and I knew this was not who I was. I learned I had to be careful before I spoke and to be gentler with my words because the unfiltered words were so abrupt and insensitive.

My two children were very important to me, so I stayed for a time with their father, because I forgot the circumstances that had brought me to the catatonic state. A new job opportunity came up for him and he was promoted to regional treasurer for a big concrete company. The new position required us to move to Charlotte, North Carolina. We were there for two years until his embezzlement from this company began to surface. I had no knowledge of his situation. I was living a life raising two children and focusing on them. He was living a double life, as I found out, being married to me in Charlotte and having an apartment in Atlanta with his gay lover. My world came tumbling down again. By God's grace, Jim made sure we returned to Dallas before law enforcement came down on him. We were safe in the home of his parents, who cared for us during this traumatic, emotional time.

At this point, I had to move on as I could not continue living a life of deceit. Even though I did not know everything that Jim was doing, we had been victims of his lifestyle. This was not the life I could support any longer. I stayed longer in the marriage than I should have because of our two children, but I could not allow their lives to be influenced by lies and betrayals. My daughter, at four years old, begged me not to leave him, but I knew she did not understand there were certain boundaries and morals I had to live by. Lies and deceit were not among them, so we divorced. At twenty-five years old, I had to grow up and take responsibility as a single mom of two young children.

I found a job working at a bank making $450 a month. This was back in the 1970s, and during these years on my own, I look back and do not know how we survived. I did have help from my ex-husband's family as well as my own. My aunt helped me buy a car that cost $60 a month. My father-in-law always worried about us having enough to eat, so he brought groceries every week. I was grateful for all the support. Through all this, I realized I was searching for something outside of myself to find Love. I had allowed fear to run my life through my own ignorance and lack of awareness. I have come to learn that this is one of our big mishaps in life. If you think Love is outside of yourself, then you may be searching for a while, always thinking you found love and realizing in the end that love, disguised as fear, betrayed you.

I was not aware of my spiritual journey yet, but I kept moving forward. I knew I had to search for something deeper and more meaningful than what I had experienced to that point. There was a dim light within me that encouraged me to keep going, and I did. As fate would have it, that was not what Spirit had intended for my life, but I experienced the reality of my first marriage to know the difference between love and fear. Later, I realized that what I lived through in my younger years was very valuable for me to help others in the future having experienced the depth of despair, lack, and all the insecurities. Having lived all of this, I would be empathetic to those people going through what I had. I would be able to understand where they were and why they were there. The enlightenment of understanding my past experiences that were fear-based and taking me further from Love helped me to reframe my life into focusing on what I wanted instead of what I did not want. The blessing on the other side is that truth will always set you free if you are open to receiving it. This experience began the journey of searching higher within myself. Something stronger within me kept growing, and I know now that it was my spirit that drove me to keep searching; to keep growing. I did not know where it would lead, but I believed that life had better experiences to elevate me to a more welcoming place. I became open to new knowledge and growth, as I wanted to leave behind the world that did not seem to fit me anymore.

What I learned is that the most in-depth relationships come from finding love first within yourself, and then love will come to you in many forms. If I had known this earlier, I would have made different decisions. I did not have any clue at the time that I was the key to my own success and the value of what I wanted. No one had taught me this. I had to discover the secrets on my own, through my life's journeys. I had to stumble through life until I had enough. When I was ready to discover this, Spirit came into my life. This happened when I said I couldn't do this life anymore without some sort of fulfillment that was supported by Love. I needed something to bring depth into why I was even here. "Why am I here? What meaning do I have in my life?" I asked. I wanted to know.

With these questions I asked of Spirit, my life began a new adventure of seeking Love and truth. Moving forward, my journey to find the depths of Love guided me to my first spiritual teacher, Carla Gordan. My life forever changed because she taught me more than Love and its nature; she also made me aware of the belief system that we create from our life experiences and what is drawn to us is from this belief system that influences our lives.

I learned that when I felt I was at the bottom, at the end of my marriage, I had a fear-based belief system that was not supporting my life. This was a time I had nowhere else to go but up. Whatever that place may be for you, it is a time to look within, to reflect on your life, to open yourself for clarity, and to ask questions for guidance. Even if you don't know, your soul knows your destiny. This became a time for me to connect within and listen to my soul. Ask and you shall receive.

What has your life taught you so far about Love and fear? I am hoping you are on the same path of discovering who you really are, because fear only leads to dead ends. The dead ends become very weary of your effort to continue to support them.

Healing Love Practice

The Awareness

Self-love is the ultimate journey in finding yourself.

When has your life felt like ground zero and you had
to reach deep to move toward something better?

When do you feel Love dwelling within to inspire your life?

My Affirmation

The Love that dwells within me grows
and expands to guide me on my journey.

CHAPTER 3

The Spiritual World Awakens

Carla Gordan was a spiritual teacher I was introduced to after I had traveled down every road of disaster; lacking direction, spinning my wheels, and not going anywhere in my life. Fear was the driver of my life until I met her. Carla was a trance medium, a Doctor of Divinity and Metaphysics and an ordained minister. My first introduction to Carla's work was in 1983. I had a reading from her with my sister sitting in as a proxy for me, asking questions I had written for her to ask on my behalf. I was very impressed with the accuracy of the answers that were given. I had the reading transcribed from a cassette tape that was given to me after the reading. I had not met Carla, and yet there was a connection of spiritual insight that was given. My curiosity grew, as I knew there was something intriguing and mysterious about this information that was so accurate.

I discovered that Carla had workshops that she called "Intensives." These were weekend workshops that usually had twelve to fifteen people and began on a Friday evening, followed by a full day Saturday, and ended with a half day on Sunday. Carla did these "Intensives" in many parts of the country. The first Intensive I attended in 1983 was in her home, and it massively altered my perceptions of life. The Friday evening session was focused on teaching us spiritual principles and Love. I was absorbing all of it as if it was fresh air to my soul. Carla ended the evening with a trance session for our group. This session brought together the reason we were all drawn together and the theme for the weekend. At the end of the evening, I felt like Christmas had come early, and could not wait until the next day.

The purpose of the first session on Saturday was to align us all with a spiritual foundation and principles that were like the Ten Commandments, written in stone, and yet rang so true to my soul. "There is only Love" was the first and foremost truth I learned from her in the beginning. During the day we had one-on-one time with her in front of the group, where she would be guided spiritually to take us back in time to certain ages; anchors in time that would direct us to what we were there to heal. She was loving and supportive, allowing us space to connect with our past. She would go into the timeline of our life, beginning at an age where the fear-based experience started and progressing forward through the years where this same fear had intersected in our lives. By the end, we understood what we had been ordained "by divine appointment" to heal. It was always a false belief and fear-based. As each person shared their experience, we learned that we had many connecting, but different, life experiences. This built a strong cohesiveness within the group.

This strong connection grew between all of us and there was love and understanding of each journey that was in pain, but love transcended each person through seeing the truth of the situation. By the end on Sunday afternoon, we had such a strong connection with each other that we felt like a new light of Love had opened within us. After spending time in a spiritual space of Love and connection, I went home and realized that my newfound awareness of Love had changed how I saw my life. This perception made me step back from interactions and experiences when I realized what I was experiencing from my outside world looked somewhat different.

I was sold on the transformation of fear into a Love energy. Overcoming my fears opened the doorway to Love and connection. I was able to feel how Love brings people together and how fear separates us. The group began as strangers, meeting for the first time, and left as a family who embraced love for each other.

What I experienced over a ten-year period of being her spiritual student was that she helped me bring to life a new spiritual version of myself that I could not have achieved on my own. I did not have the foundation to embrace it without her teachings. New spiritual gifts and talents began to unfold. This came after attending her Intensives, usually twice a year. I realized over time that the process of spending one weekend with Carla expanded and would take place for approximately four months. The fear I was preparing to heal began surfacing a couple of months before the Intensive, and a couple of months afterward, the spiritual lessons were processed and implemented into my life.

Carla taught me about spiritual energy, my guides who were with me, and that I was much more than my earlier beliefs in life. Over this period, going to her Intensives, many barriers and chains were broken that had weighed me down emotionally. I transformed my inner house built with sand to a house built with a foundation of Love that felt like a solid stone structure. There was no doubt in my mind that Love was the only answer to fear.

My spiritual energies were enhanced as I grew within this foundation of Love. I recognized I could see images and hear the spiritual world giving me messages. I was invited by spirit to take this out for a spin and see what happened, as if I was stepping into a new car and wanted to experience the feel of it on the road. I was a massage therapist then, and I practiced implementing energy work with the massages I gave. As I blended the two, I was aware of messages I was receiving as I worked with different areas of massaging a client's body. I experienced more energy spikes and messages when I was around the neck, head, and arms. The energy flowing through the arms was opening energy for giving and receiving. The left arm is the energy receiver, and the right arm is the energy that gives outwardly. I could detect resistances with the flow of their energy as I worked with them. If someone was experiencing tightness in their neck, I would receive messages or images of the resistance they were holding. As I became more connected with working with these energies, I began to share with the person who was receiving the body/energy work what I was seeing or hearing. I found they confirmed what I shared was true, or they realized the truth in what I was seeing shortly thereafter.

Word of mouth spread, and I never had to advertise to receive new clients. Bringing the spiritually-guided energy to massage gave an enhanced outcome of how people would feel in their body and energy field afterward. This happened for me in the 1980s, and by the early 1990s, I received a call from a physical therapist one day telling me that she had a patient who had received all the traditional treatment they knew to give her. This patient had continuous migraines and was desperately trying to find relief after being in a car wreck two years earlier. She knew I was somewhat "outside the box" of traditional medicine, but nothing in physical therapy could relieve any of her symptoms, so I accepted the challenge to see if there was anything I could do to help.

The woman came to my clinic with her husband, and I had her lie down on my treatment table. I asked to be spiritually guided through this as I, by myself, had no idea how to help her beyond what treatment she had received. Her neck was too sensitive to touch, so I was drawn to her left hand. I was guided to pressure points in her hand, and I allowed spirit to flow through me and let spirit take over. I observed that as these pressure points were being applied, there was a high flow of energy coming through. With light massage, the pressure points progressed upward to her forearm very gently. The left arm began to open to receiving as it progressed from her forearm to her arm. By the time my hands were at her shoulder, I slowly and carefully laid my hands on her neck. I felt a flow of spiritual energy of Love flowing through my hands into her neck. My hands gently embraced her neck, and slight pressure was placed to elongate the neck to free the energy locked inside. Once the treatment was over, I helped her sit up. The next day she returned with excitement, stating that it was the first time in two years she did not have a migraine. For the second treatment, I worked with her neck to stretch and regain flexibility, and then she was complete.

The evolution of Spirit on Earth grows continually as we receive blessings from this connection. My life has been forever blessed with the spiritual foundation received from Carla and her teachings. The insight that can be gained through our connection with the spiritual world is priceless. The beauty of knowing there is always more growth from learning through new experiences we have not participated in yet, can make us excited about the future and what it will bring.

Healing Love Practice

The Awareness

The connection of Love gives blessings we pass on to others.

How has abiding in Love given unexpected gifts?
What teacher has given insights to your love connections?

My Affirmation

Love is a bridge to my connection with life.

CHAPTER 4

The Courage to Pursue a New Career

Career changes are scary when you are completely out of your wheel-house and have no reference to anything like the new journey you are embarking upon. Fear can play some powerful games with your mind and emotions. Fear will pull out so much, so quickly, that you don't know what hit you. Fear's mission is to hold you back and to keep you from moving forward. Fear does not want you to grow or experience new things that might elevate you or empower you. All those hidden wounds begin to surface to make you feel insecure, like you are not enough, and to hold you back from an attempt or a dream to move forward.

Sometimes, going for a career change can be more challenging than fun. Your life is daring you to take the challenge; you feel your spirit inspiring you to do so and the synchronicity of it all melts together, and it is hard to resist. I had never envisioned myself going into the medical field, but there it was before me. My best friend, who was my comrade in navigating our spiritual lives together, told me one day, "Linda, you are such a great massage therapist, you should pursue a career in physical therapy."

I was living in Galveston at the time, and the University of Texas Medical Branch (UTMB) was a thriving force on the island. I was working for them already in an area of time keeping for the employees of the hospital. That was a pretty boring job, but I needed employment when I had just married and moved to the area.

As I contemplated the possibilities, I decided to check out the college requirements to apply for the physical therapy program. I would need two years of college courses to fulfill their requirements at the time, so I decided to go for it. Going into a junior college on the island was awkward at first because of my age. I was thirty-two years old. Most people thought going back to college at my age was too old, but I did it anyway. My husband was big on higher education and supported my choice. I was afraid and reluctant at first, but then flowed with the happiness of learning and growing.

When you apply to a physical therapy school your grade point average (GPA) means everything. I completed my two years with a 3.8 GPA, not the best, but good enough that when I submitted my application, I received an acceptance letter in the mail, and I was overjoyed! The school requires 150 hours of working in a physical therapy setting as one of their requirements. I went to the Transitional Learning Center to get my hours. I worked with the physical therapist in the rehab portion of their late training for head injuries and helping patients get back into the community. Jody Tomberlin was the female therapist who took me under her wing. I learned, after my acceptance into the program, that her referral was probably my ticket in, as she used to be on the faculty there and they all knew her. That particular year, they did not do interviews because of the new health science building that had just been completed. Our class was the first to be in the new building.

Stepping back a moment, the fact that I was navigated to Jody at the Transitional Learning Center was definitely spiritually guided. When you move beyond the fears that present themselves, you get rewarded. She was my first mentor in the world of physical therapy. She noticed how I was so interested in the people there that had experienced head injuries and how I interacted with them that she asked me one day, "Are you sure you want to be a physical therapist instead of a psychologist?"

I assured her that physical therapy was what I wanted. I had always been curious about how each patient felt during their recovery from their brain injury.

I was very excited about my physical therapy career until I attended my first class. I thought to myself, "What did I just get myself into?"

From the first day, I knew this road was going to challenge and test every ounce of intelligence. I thought, "But I am intuitive and spiritual. How am I going to survive this?"

I took one semester at a time. I got tutors for certain areas that my mind was struggling to embrace. Memorizing was not one of my strong suits, but I had to do it anyway. I struggled many times during the course of completing the classes.

During all this, I continued going to Intensives with Carla, my spiritual teacher, and pursuing my spiritual growth. Much of my growth was about being intelligent enough, being strong enough, being good enough to see this program through. It all seemed to be about being enough through a strange, new area of physical mechanics, more so than inspiration. I had to dig deep during these times to get through.

One of the most enlightening things I heard was from one of our faculty members as we were coming closer to our clinical exams. She said to the class that some of the most average students' grade-wise made some of the best clinicians out in the field. My ears perked up because I knew she was talking about me, and it turned out to be true. In our clinicals, I shined because I connected so easily with patients and my spirit was with me to help them in a positive way. My connections with people were strong and appreciation always followed. I was happy once I graduated and had a job before graduation in an outpatient clinic.

Starting anything new is challenging in the beginning and rewarding in the end if you are where you are supposed to be. In our lives we want to be comfortable, but sometimes we have to step out of our comfort zone to go for something better. Challenge comes knocking at our door in life to see if we are open to grow and pursue more. Personally, many members of my family thought I would fail or give up. That gave me a stronger drive to make it through, so they were really my cheerleaders. It does not matter what drives you. It is your inner force that will prevail. I am grateful for spirit guiding me toward this career that has allowed me to serve so many people for over thirty-five years. I have experienced many amazing cases, but there are a few that stood out during my time in home health that gave me my wings.

The home health agency called me one morning concerning a patient who had recently suffered a stroke. I was reluctant in the beginning to take the case because I had spent two years in an outpatient clinic and did not feel that I had the experience. I decided to see if there was anything I could do to help. I went to the patient's home for the evaluation and met with the woman lying in a hospital bed that was set up in their dining room. Her facial expression showed me she was afraid. Her husband was there, and I talked to both of them. I learned that the doctor had sent her home and told her she would be bedridden for the rest of her life, so she did not qualify for rehab. Spirit was very much guiding me, as I had asked for help to guide me through this time with her. Not knowing what I could do to help her, I directed my attention back to her and asked, "What do you want?"

She replied, "I want to walk again."

I felt a very strong connection and conviction in her response, so I said, "Okay. There will be a lot of work and challenges. Are you willing to do the work to get there?"

She responded, "Yes!"

I said, "Okay, let's do it."

I started with helping her to sit unsupported. I asked Spirit to guide me with the skills I needed to help her. The work was tedious and took patience, but she was one hundred percent present and willing every time I worked with her. Everything I asked her to do, she did her best to go through all of the challenges we faced, and she began to show improvement. I was guided with my knowledge that I was using from my physical therapy education, but also with Spirit being present and guiding me where to take her next. Weeks became months, but this beautiful patient kept making progress. We were at the point of working on standing. This was rough in the beginning, but she never gave up. I admired her strength and courage to move through the impossible to claim what she wanted.

I ordered her a bilateral platform walker that was delivered to her home. By then she was able to transfer easily to her wheelchair. I took her into the family room of her home with her husband there. We had the platform walker, a gait belt around her waist, and I had her stand. Her husband was about fifteen feet away and in front of her. The smile on her face was huge as she took steps for the first time since her stroke. This was an exciting moment for all of us. As she walked toward her husband, I couldn't help but feel the gratitude within me for helping her achieve this. What she wanted, she achieved. Fifteen feet may be a small distance for some, but for her, and the rest of us, it was huge!

When I left her, she had been accepted into physical rehab because of the progress she had made at home. This was a journey I took on feeling very insecure due to my lack of experience with stroke patients. What I learned is, if I have a willing patient, we can do miracles together. The will and determination she demonstrated allowed the chains to break the prognosis from her doctor to be bedbound for the rest of her life. She defied the odds through her persistence and will to destroy the boundaries of her limitations, and in pursuing her goal against all odds, she achieved what she wanted.

When you witness something like that, you have to ask yourself, "What would I do if I had nothing to lose and everything to gain?" I was so deeply grateful for the experience. I felt that her spirit and mine were very connected, and together helped us work out the mechanics of what needed to be done each session I worked with her. This was a *WOW* moment of achievement that confirmed I was where I was meant to be.

There was another home health assignment I was given that was very near the same thing. The difference was that he had been in ICU for a month. He was the mayor of a small town. I went to his home, and he was lying in his bed. I introduced myself and had no idea what he was able to do. He was an amputee, and had a prosthesis for his left leg that he had used prior to the hospitalization. I sat beside his bed to talk to him. He looked at me and asked sincerely, "Do you think I will ever get better?"

At that moment, I had to see him whole again. I responded to him, "Yes, absolutely, you will get stronger."

He was another one who was so weak that he could barely sit on the edge of the bed. I guarded him in the beginning because he fatigued quickly. It was a slow process, but every time I came, we worked on building his endurance and strength. We worked on his ability to walk again with a walker. The time came for me to work with him on his balance and reuniting him with his prosthesis. This is when I asked Spirit for help. I had not been taught this in school. I led him to walk to his kitchen counter and then I began to teach him exercises to balance and bear weight through his prosthesis. These were visions that came to me, breaking down components that allowed the hips and lower extremities to stabilize during weight bearing on one leg at a time. He followed every step I asked of him. I was in a flow of Spirit, balance, and teaching. He was courageous as he followed every cue and instruction I gave. After many sessions of training, he walked confidently through his home with stability and strength that he did not have when we first started. I had done my job indoors, but then I asked him, "What did you always do outside your home that you have not done since all this happened?"

He responded, "I always loved to go to the lake and fish."

I said, "On our next session, I want you to take me to that place."

It was a perfect time to offer a session with altered terrain compared to the flat surfaces in his home. I wanted to help him get back to the life he had before the hospital and ICU experience. He took me to a nearby lake, and as a physical therapist I noticed right away that there were inclines and uneven surfaces that he would have to navigate. He navigated these challenges well by using the balance exercises I had taught him. I was pleased that I had brought him home to the life he loved and that he could continue. He was very grateful, and I was too! My mission as a physical therapist to break through the limitations imposed by an illness or a prolonged hospitalization was rewarding because I got to help patients regain strength, resume their favorite hobbies, and live normal lives again.

There was a different patient who was referred to me who had a hard start in life because she was born three months premature. I had been asked by the state of Arkansas, which I contracted with, to help her developmental skills to catch up with her age. I first thought, "Oh my God, I have never really worked with a baby."

But then I reflected back on my stroke patient who was supposed to be bedridden and who I had helped to walk again. I took the case, and when I got there, she was six months old and did not know how to roll over. Again, I called on Spirit to help me with this baby. As I began to work with her, I felt every step I needed to do to progress her. We went from her discovering how to roll from her back onto her stomach and then back again. I worked with her from lying down to coming to a sitting position. We worked on sitting balance and she was able to sit independently. This happened over months.

I realized that she had been ready, she only needed to be shown the way. Her parents were overjoyed with her progress. I would always leave instructions on how to help reinforce our sessions until my next visit.

When she was thirteen months old, I taught her how to crawl. The moment came to teach her to stand. She had done so well with catching up with her developmental skills up to that point. I was so proud of her, and I could tell how proud she was to learn all the new skills that helped her to be more mobile. She began her first steps supported by holding on to my fingers or the coffee table. Once I got her to that point, I guided her parents to progress her. She was a beautiful child and so focused on catching up that I was in awe of her courage.

I have not seen these patients since I left them. I recognized, during my time with them, how much I admired their inner courage to achieve beyond what life had handed them. They were the ones who believed and had hope beyond their limitations. I was deeply grateful for being a part of their journey. Their desire to reach for a higher level than what they experienced in their weakest moments gave me inspiration for my own life to have that same courage to move through my own limitations. When you have nothing to lose and everything to gain, life will help you move mountains when your heart has the passion to achieve what seems to be impossible.

You don't have to be a physical therapist to influence other people's lives. We do it all the time; sometimes not even knowing the extent of how much we are helping. Whenever you care about another's life and you add value to their experience, you have given an enlightening participation in what they will take within and remember. When have you experienced a life changing event because you gave of yourself or were given something that helped you forward toward what you were seeking? Life is a journey, and many times it asks us to move through the unknown and uncertainties to achieve something new that will bring value to our lives both now and in the future.

Healing Love Practice

The Awareness

We develop what will allow us to serve.

What have you experienced where you had to go outside
your comfort zone to receive amazing results?

What motivated the desire and inner
drive to overcome the obstacles?

My Affirmation

I Am the courage and strength to overcome any obstacles.

CHAPTER 5

Healing the Racial Divide

One of my last clinicals before completing the physical therapy program was at Dallas Rehab for Spinal Cord Injuries in 1988. This clinical rotation specialized in the rehabilitation of quadriplegics and paraplegics. I came to understand the needs of these patients who were normal and "able-bodied" before their accident but left them either quadriplegic (arms and legs involved) or paraplegic (legs involved) depending on the level of their spinal cord injury. Their lives were suddenly and forever changed, for there was no repair for this type of injury. They were forced into a new and different way of life which took a great deal of mental, physical, and emotional rehabilitation to help them adjust.

The athletic director at the time was Abu Yilla. He, also, was in a wheelchair, not from a spinal cord injury, but from polio when he was a child of three years old. He had a very interesting story about his family, who lived in Sierra Leone, Africa when he was a child. When he developed polio, his father took him to England for treatment. While Abu was receiving treatment, his father went to a university and became a barrister (lawyer). I was always inspired by his story as it showed me what is possible with uniquely impossible situations. Abu remained in England and as he grew older went on to become very involved with wheelchair sports, especially basketball. What brought him to the United States was the opportunity to play for the Dallas Wheelchair Mavericks. All of this opened a new door for me, as I did not know these kinds of sports existed.

When I first met Abu, I was impressed with his level of confidence being in a wheelchair. He was an African man with an English accent who was very strong with his upper body yet unable to move his legs. Abu, as I came to learn, was an inspiration to all the spinal cord injury patients who witnessed him in action and realized their lives were not over. There is life to be lived in a wheelchair. I was strongly drawn to him and felt a heart connection. He was very intelligent and had a strong-willed, but sensitive, heart. His character was very genuine in nature. As time went on during that clinical, those feelings grew stronger. I was drawn to everything that he had become; even though he was handicapped he was one of the most "abled-bodied" people I had ever met. Even though his legs were not functional, his spirit, mind, emotional intelligence, and physical upper body were above average.

After many dates, we fell in love and wanted to be together. The problem was that my family, being Caucasian, was from the old-school mentality that Whites do not date or marry Blacks, and there were no exceptions. I was in a dilemma with my heart and my family. I knew if they only met and got to know him, they would see beyond the color of his skin and realize he was a beautiful soul and a genuine man whom I loved. That did not happen. My very conservative father was taken aback and said that he wanted to leave the state if anyone in his family found out. He was ashamed, but that was the social space he lived in. For myself, I was shocked by my family's opinions about a man who they had not ever met, except for my children and my sister. I learned what true prejudice looks like. Abu had the greatest influence on my youngest son, whom I had taught to look beyond skin color at a young age. Billy loved their time together, as Abu taught him the skill of Nintendo. Abu also taught him about reading and creating which inspired him to be a writer later down the road.

I was separated from my family during that time except for my children. The interesting discovery that I made during our relationship and our marriage was that family and friends either saw race (skin color) differences or that he was a paraplegic and in a wheelchair as a barrier. That woke me up to the reality of the consciousness of the world. I was very happy to meet his family, who welcomed me so graciously. Abu and I went to spend a long weekend with his family, gathering for a wonderful connection. I was blessed that they so embraced me, and I wished that my family could have done the same for him.

Abu introduced me to friends and couples he knew. I noticed that the couples I met were like Abu and myself. There would be one in a wheelchair and the other would be a person without disabilities. These were very warm and friendly people who were either married or dating. They lived their lives like any other normal couple.

I watched a Dallas Wheelchair Mavericks basketball game and was so impressed by the talent of the men in these wheelchairs. There was one game that I watched that was a fundraiser. The Wheelchair Mavericks played the opposing team, who were able-bodied people. The people on the other team, who were not in wheelchairs, were given two points for each basket they made to the Wheelchair Mavericks' one point. I was in disbelief as I watched the Mavericks win the game, even with their disadvantage of point scoring.

I was with Abu when he decided to try out for the Paralympic games being held that year in Seoul, Korea. I attended some of his training at a college campus on the track fields. I was amazed at his level of athleticism and knew that he loved competitive sports. He excelled in them. I was very excited for him when he made his journey to Seoul to compete. He brought home a bronze medal for one of his races. Everyone was so excited for him. He lived his life to the fullest and introduced me to a world that I cherished.

I observed Abu living his life like an able-bodied person. He would not park in a disabled parking space as he saw himself very able-bodied to go the extra distance into a restaurant if we were eating out. He washed and dried his own clothes and put them away. He drove his car with hand controls installed, loaded his wheelchair, and got in and out of his car independently. Although he was considered handicapped, he was more able-bodied than many people I knew who had legs to walk and were capable of more but did much less.

The racial divide goes both ways. As long as we look at skin color to form a conclusion without truly connecting with the heart of each individual, we lose. I sent my son to a racially integrated school in Galveston because I wanted him to learn at a young age that connecting from the heart is the truest connection you will ever find, no matter the other person's skin color. That is why he saw Abu as a mentor and a being of heart and how they truly connected. Billy, even to this day at forty-two years old, holds the utmost respect for Abu and what he taught him as a child.

What I had to experience with Billy and his father was that his father did not approve of Billy being with my husband. He never met Abu, but he did have an opinion about Billy interacting with Abu when he was with me. His father never witnessed the level of creativity that Abu was teaching Billy. There was only prejudice on the part of Billy's dad. Barriers are fear-based, and that is what our being together brought to so many of my family members. Surprisingly enough, I learned that my two older children had more challenges with Abu being in a wheelchair than being Black. The rest of the family could not get beyond his skin color. What a mess I created for being in love! I had no idea that the meaning of a person's life had so much to do with skin color or being in a wheelchair. I felt blindsided for being in a spiritually enlightened space. I stepped back to understand that this was the mindset they were in, and I could do nothing to change their opinions.

Billy's father challenged him one night as I sat at the table to talk about our situation with my marriage. His father told Billy that if he lived with me during my marriage to Abu, he would not be his father anymore. That is when I lost it and yelled, "How dare you say that to your son!"

I became so angry with the prejudiced injustice of the whole conversation. I no longer knew how to help Billy and the situation at hand. I felt bad for Billy being a young boy who was now learning about racial prejudice. This was a true, but sad, journey to move through.

My marriage to Abu lasted a short time and ended months after his best friend was hit by a car and killed one evening while crossing a busy intersection at the UT Arlington campus. Abu retreated within himself and he was unable to move beyond his best friend's sudden death. At that time, circumstances required me to move closer to my work that was across town and an hour's commute each way. After a year, I was weary of the travel every weekday, and working ten hours a day did not help. I thought that relocating would help Abu find peace in a different environment and allow me to be closer to work. I attempted to help Abu find closure with Andy's death, but as hard as I tried, I was unable to penetrate the walls that were created after his friend's death. There was now a distance that had grown between us, and I knew Abu was miserable being out of his environment and away from the friends he loved. We both became miserable over a few months, and we made the difficult decision to part ways.

Abu did not share the same spiritual beliefs that I had, and my attempts to comfort him were not helpful. After Andy's death, I felt Andy's spirit attempting to reach Abu, but his heart was closed. His friend was unable to connect or communicate with him. I felt that Andy's freedom with being whole again after his death was exciting for him, to be free from the body that was quadriplegic and limited to a wheelchair.

As years have passed, we have grown as a society to be accepting of an array of skin colors, but interracial marriages that were not as prevalent back in the late '80s or early '90s. I have taken notice that even cousins within my father's family now have interracial marriages and children of their own from these marriages. This is refreshing to see.

The prejudices and limitations of our minds are opening to see the true spirit that lives within each individual no matter their race, culture, or disability. This has been one of our human growth assignments, to open our minds and hearts to heal these limitations. This awareness has helped me understand the spirit that dwells in each person. No matter the color of their skin or if there is a disability that limits their body, we can overcome the barriers to see the true spirit within.

This part of my life opened my eyes to many things. Abu introduced me into a world that I would have never experienced if our paths had not crossed. I feel blessed by our short but enriched journey together. He is a person I admire for his inner strength to live life on his own terms. I have continued, throughout the years, to be inspired by his accomplishments in life and always wish him well.

Has your life intersected with another, no matter the differences, where your life was enhanced by the wealth you received from the time together? As we explore and open to new journeys in life, we will be guided to areas that will inspire and raise us to new levels of awareness. We are designed to grow within and to experience new things and possibilities. No matter how old you are, keep anticipating the new, exciting adventures that life can bring you.

Healing Love Practice

The Awareness

There are no colors or disabilities of human life that are absent of God's Love.

What unique experience or encounter has given your life more depth and meaning?

How many times have you been given the opportunity to see beyond the surface?

The Affirmation

I see the beauty within each soul on Earth.

CHAPTER 6

Seeing the World
Through New Lenses

Love and fear influence what we see or miss seeing every day. The more connected we are to our inner self-love, the more we notice special moments where our vision can grasp something unique and distinctive that we can take inside us and appreciate. Fear distracts us from seeing the beauty that surrounds us by its diversion of negativity, what's not right, and self-absorption of non-relevant issues of the past. Yet, self-awareness heightens the quality of what we see and experience. Fear relishes in the delight of limiting and narrowing our vision to focus on the part of what went wrong, the horrible nightmare of being let down, or what life is keeping from us.

Sometimes, life can become mundane to the point we stop noticing details. Every day, we see visually what is happening in front of us any time we are paying attention. Details of what we see are what can help us pick up on distress, when someone needs support or kindness, or when someone is excited and happy. These are varying emotions that we can see visually. From our eyes, we can see when someone is having a great day or being challenged. The outer world is a direct connection for us if we notice, see, or even respond to it. If we see and connect with it, allows us to respond or just pass by and let it go.

As spiritual awareness grows, so does your vision of what you see.

Your spiritual awareness raises your vibrational energy that, in turn, enhances your vision of what you see. This higher energy allows you to notice the loving qualities in a person. You notice a new depth to the person you had not been aware of before. The beauty you are seeing in them reflects your own inner beauty. When you see someone, you don't know, or who is on the street that is homeless, what does this reflect? This was my assignment from the spiritual world that asked me to venture out in my daily life to find the answer to this question for myself.

I was living on Galveston Island with my family and attending physical therapy school and pursing my spiritual journeys. One day my spirit proposed an idea, and I listened. What if you could look beyond everyone's physical body and see the light of their soul no matter what their physical body demonstrated or what appeared on the surface? I thought for a moment and realized I would love that. As I practiced, I was amazed to see how we cannot judge people by their bodies and what they do when we see their soul. I practiced seeing the homeless with hunched over backs, looking as if their body was carrying a heavy load. Then I reached into my higher vision that revealed their true spirit, and it was always so beautiful to see and witness. I saw people whose physical face told me that they were feeling so heavy that they could not smile. Again, my higher vision showed me that their spirits were radiant. I became aware through my continual practice of this with every stranger passing by that I encountered that this three-dimensional world limits our vision immensely. The world we see with our physical vision is so out of sync with our true spirit. Spiritual vision gave me far greater insight into the true soul of each individual.

Why did spirit want me to experience this? I believe these encounters were for my awareness to see and feel the differences of the two visions. With physical vision comes automatic conclusions and judgements. With spiritual vision comes a higher vibration of insight into the beauty of the soul, two completely different experiences. These people were not friends or acquaintances, they were random people who I did not know that I saw on the street or passed in hallways. My question to spirit was, "What if the whole world could see with their spiritual vision?"

And Spirit replied:

How do you see things that others cannot? Spiritual vision is another dimension of sight. You are not looking through the eyes that were given to you from the earth. It is a higher vibration of vision that can only be seen through your sensitivity. You must be in a state of Love and appreciation of life.

I then realized that most of the people in the world weren't there yet, but that was continually changing. Global fear presented itself with Covid in 2020, which showed us that the world can shift and change in a heartbeat. Fear was the driver in this pandemic. I had never witnessed a global drive of fear of this magnitude until that time. You either isolated yourself or you went deeper into yourself to define its meaning for you. I reached deeper into Love and away from the fear that was circulating with great intensity. I wanted a higher awareness spiritually of all the fear and isolation that was all around me. From my spiritual vision, I could see a world in such panic and fear that I knew my part was to stay balanced and loving to those who were in fear. I had to see Covid from a different perspective. I communicated with spirit often to keep my perspective of Love and compassion as I worked with many patients in the hospital who were trying to survive this deadly virus.

The world sometimes teaches me that I need to tone down my spirit because it makes others too uncomfortable. They know about it but haven't delved deeply into it. Their physical world, what appears to be real, has more precedence. I understand the dynamics of what is happening. This is what makes the earth so beautiful. We are all given choices of what we want to believe and experience. Some of my happiest times are being with my spiritual friends. I feel love, acceptance, and support from our friendship. We are free to be who we are and accepted as that. There are no judgment or expectations.

No one is perfect. I have my moments where I slide momentarily, caught off guard, into a fear reaction, a trigger that ignites my emotion, and catch it. Sometimes it is quick and sometimes I have to reflect on it. Self-awareness assists with the process. There are times when someone says something that hurts my feelings. When there is a fear-based reaction, these are times that I must process. What did they say that hurt me and what made it hurt so deeply? That is when I switch visions emotionally. I tune out of Earth vision and reach into my spiritual vision for the truth of why I was impacted by their words. I must be honest with my emotions and let go of judgment and pride. Spiritual vision only sees the truth of the reality of your experience. With this truth, you find the deficit within yourself that created it. I find my belief that made me feel hurt. I was momentarily responsible for their life and happiness. I got caught in a momentary illusion that sucked me right in. The beauty is that you can let it go once you understand the meaning behind it. There is no way I can be responsible for anyone's life or happiness but my own.

There is a deeper aspect to this. What is my attachment to this person that I care for so deeply that I would never want to be the cause of pain in their life? Earth vision would cause me to see the emotional upset and I am responsible because I brought something that has possibilities of limiting this person's joy. What I find is an attachment emotionally to this person. This is from my spiritual vision. I could not get to this in my physical vision. You are so emotionally attached to this person and this person to you that you play these dynamics back and forth to each other, and then you forgive and life goes on until the next time, when it could be the other way around. "How do I heal from this?" I asked my spirit.

With ones who are deeply connected in Love, it is easy to be entrapped with believing you are responsible for each other's happiness and joy. Take within your spirit to see the higher vision of your deep love for this soul. Give them understanding that they are also human, and they will have their own ups and downs in life. Hold the beauty of their spirit in your heart in their down times to love and support what they are experiencing, not to take as your own. Love and support, not attaching any earthly component to the experience. You can be mirrors to one another. What hurts one hurts the other. Look in the mirror and take within your being what the other is reflecting into your mirror. You will see that the reflection with the other is how you are feeling as the cause. This comes as a belief that you can create a circumstance that can cause another pain.

What is the true lesson here? The answers are within your being when you learn to connect with your spirit. All of the answers to your life lives within you. As a holistic life coach, I learned to hold the higher vision of the person before me to help them find their own answers. This is to empower them to know that when they can connect with their spirit, the answers are there for them. My spiritual journey has been ongoing through most of my adult life. What spirit has enhanced is how I see the world, how I feel about the world, and how I embrace the world. I coach to enhance other souls' journeys to a higher vision of the world for those who are open to receive.

Another way that spirit taught me to see with my spiritual vision was seeing something so uniquely small and yet so magnificent when witnessed. You are there with your Earth vision and you might notice and appreciate the green grass as you walk on it, but there is never a thought that there is life within it. This is what I experienced through my spiritual vision. There was a time I will never forget, and it seemed so insignificant in the beginning. I was looking down at the grass and my bare feet where I happened to be with friends on a warm spring afternoon. I was admiring and appreciating the grass as I was bending and releasing my toes in it. I began to focus on one blade of grass. I did not understand why I was drawn to this, but I was. I focused on it for a moment, and suddenly it showed me the radiance of life within itself. I was in awe of what I was seeing. This one blade was showing me an illuminating white light radiating around it. A true, life force in a blade of grass. When you see the life force vibrating through a blade of grass, you understand the power of the forces of energy that is God. Nothing is insignificant that was created by the Source of all Creation. I realized later that the admiration and appreciation of the grass beneath my feet lifted me into my spiritual vision to experience the life force that, for many people, would have very little meaning at all. I thought to myself, *if I can see this, what other things of nature and beauty are waiting for me to discover them?*

My journey at Alan Cohen's first Mastery Training in 1993 demonstrated my spiritual vision and trusting the lead of my spirit. At that time, Alan took us to the Seven Sacred Falls in Maui. We journeyed underneath the falls that many do not tend to go to. Alan did not know where we were going, and everyone kept following my lead. I was leading the group, like I knew where I was going even though I had never been to this place before. I had no idea, but I followed spirit and my inner vision. It was a fun journey of anticipation and excitement of not knowing where we were being led, but we kept moving forward. I kept swimming and picking up speed with a sense we were coming close, until we arrived at this grand archway. I said, "This is it!"

We all entered this sacred space that spirit had reserved just for us. There was no one else that ventured as deep into the underground as we did that day. Beyond this magnificent stone archway was a tall, slender, but powerfully flowing waterfall high above the stone walls that built this dome; an enclosure that felt like sacred ground, flowing its water from the waterfall into the pool that surrounded us. It was enchanting. We were swimming, having fun, and enjoying our innocence, playing like children. The time came for us to leave, and we all felt renewed, relaxed, and happy. Alan quoted Buddha to our group as we were making our journey back, "Only those who go where few have gone can see what few have seen."

We were all on a spiritual high from that experience.

There have undoubtedly been times when you have seen something that was an aha moment, something that touched your inner spirit. It captured your heart's awareness of something unique and different from anything you have experienced. That was your spirit hinting to you that there is more than what is the norm of Earth. You see subtle hints from your vision that spirit slides in when least expected to give you a glimmer of another dimension of life. As we continue to move toward our inner healing of old wounds or beliefs that no longer serve us, we open our ability to draw adventures that will uplift and expand our inner world that we are nurturing.

Healing Love Practice

The Awareness

**Spiritual vision is a higher level of insight
than that of the human world.**

What have you seen that does not fit
with a three-dimensional world?

Has a multidimensional awareness
changed your world of possibilities?

My Affirmation

I see through the lenses of Love that see the truth.

CHAPTER 7

Synchronicities Bring Unexpected Gifts

Synchronicity, or coincidence as many view it, can come into our life at unexpected moments that offer a connection, an insight, or opportunities, and the result is having an uplifting experience that leaves you feeling amazed. Synchronicities draw people to the right time and place to rendezvous with an experience that is there to unite with the inner summons of the harmony of energy. This can come in the form of meeting a stranger who you instantly feel a deep connection with or an experience that gives you epiphany moments about something larger than you have ever experienced. I feel that these moments of connection, in whatever form they take, are blessings from the Universe, Spirit, or God.

I had spent about five years with Carla, and my spiritual evolution kept unfolding. I received a call from Carla one day asking if I would attend a Native American workshop at Peace Valley, the property she owned for retreats. I was very surprised and honored to do this. She had me stay in her room at no cost to me. I gathered that she wanted someone she knew to be her eyes for a first-time workshop on her property by a man who was presenting there. Peace Valley was near Gaddo Gap, Arkansas, in the Ouachita National Forest on seventy acres of land. Little did I know at the time, I was being drawn there by synchronicity or, as I learned from Carla, "by divine appointment."

Native American rituals had always intrigued me, as my soul yearned to connect and learn about them because my father's family was part of this culture. My spirit was alive with new opportunities for adventure, and I was excited. I arrived at Peace Valley and met Philip, who was leading the workshop. He did not have any resemblance to what I pictured as a Native American. He was dishwater blonde, very respectful, and easy to interact with. I was curious about where this workshop would take our small group of nine.

One morning after breakfast, Philip announced to the group that we each needed to bring a blindfold, such as a scarf or kerchief, and meet outside. He led all of us to an open, grassy field ringed by trees. We were all curious about this adventure. Our instructions were to form groups of two. One person would be blindfolded to do the walk and the other person would stay close but not interfere unless their blindfolded partner was moving toward something that might hurt them. There were an odd number of us, so Philip offered to be my partner. He applied my blindfold over my eyes and then he instructed the partners to turn us in circles a few times and let us go. I learned very quickly that I would have to use my instincts to move through the journey. Without my sight, the journey added a new element that I had not experienced before. Then we began our "trust walk."

I began to walk forward with my arms gently stretched out in front of me. I was somewhat uncomfortable at first without being able to see where I was going. I learned quickly that this journey was about trusting my intuitive self within me. I was tuning into my inner voice to guide me. Not long into the walk, I came to an abrupt halt. My inner voice of fear told me I was at the edge of a cliff, and if I took one more step, I would fall off of it. My inner vision of fear showed me the picture of where I was. My adrenaline was flowing. I hesitated for a time with an internal conflict. Philip asked me what I was experiencing, and I told him the vision I was seeing in my mind's eye. He was patient and allowed me the space to process the fear. As I was holding back the trust to take the next step, there was a gentle, loving voice internally that told me I was safe to take a step forward. I had to decide if I was going to trust what this voice said or trust my fear of falling off the cliff. I gained the courage to take that step in faith. When I took the step forward, my foot landed on solid ground. I was relieved and renewed. This was an empowering moment, as I felt that I could trust my inner voice of Love even though my fear tried to make me feel differently. The distinction of energies between the two voices allowed me to be aware of the difference. I felt safe when the voice of Love was speaking to me.

After that experience, I began to open my sensitivity and allow myself to hear the crackles of leaves and tree limbs swaying in the breeze as I stepped forward. I heard the sounds of the birds and nature begin to embrace me as I continued to walk forward. For a moment, I realized I was in a space just like my younger sister who was blind and got a feeling for how she navigated her life without sight. I became more aware of my inner being to trust, keep me safe, and to guide me through this adventure.

I began to feel comfortable allowing my spirit to guide me through my exploration in nature without my eyes. I began trusting my inner vision and what I was being moved toward. I came to a place where I was guided to sit on the ground. I could feel the sun shining on my forehead, and the warmth was very comforting as I sat down. I focused straight ahead on the sun, became relaxed in the sun's warmth, and then the vision of a snake danced across the path of my inner vision. The vision brought a story of a past life. I saw myself as a male Indian who had left the tribe feeling like I had failed the tests that were given and feeling unworthy of being in the tribe. In my heart, I felt I had failed the tribe that meant so much to me. Sitting with the warmth of the sun on my face, my heart felt compelled to surround this male Indian, who had given everything he had at the time, with love, forgiveness, and understanding that I had done my best during that time. This male Indian was unable to live with failure and hold his head up in front of the tribe. My energy continued surrounding and embracing him with love, understanding, and forgiveness. Suddenly, a tribe of Indians appeared in a circle in front of me. The chief was there with a beautiful feather headdress. He spoke to me and said, "We have come here to honor you, but we could not honor you until you had honored yourself."

It was a surreal moment. There was more love embodying me than I had ever felt. I was experiencing a realm of the spiritual world from another lifetime.

The love and connection in my heart that the whole tribe was sending me was empowering my spiritual being. The energy of the tribe faded, and my journey was complete. I took off my blindfold and looked at the sun in front of me. As I turned around, I noticed that behind me there was a huge tree that Philip called "the tree of life." The trust walk spiritually enlightened me in so many ways. I was grateful for this journey that reinforced my belief in Spirit and the energies beyond the Earth guiding my life even more. I knew I was on the right path; the path of enlightenment of spirit within. I was humbled and grateful.

Every spiritual journey kept renewing my spirit and leading me forward to the next. There was so much growth to experience once I realized that my wounds were also from other lives. This made me aware that each spirit is multi-dimensional in that our past lives can intersect with our life now.

Love is an energy of pureness with nothing opposing it. The natural being of self is always seeking to love and seeking to be loved. It is an instinct in human lives to search to experience and feel this Love that brings you home to your true spirit. We watch over you with love, knowing we are unable to interfere with what you choose in your life. We support you when you feel the pressure of fear coming into your life, only to be transformed. We help you with this and support your journey through every obstacle you encounter. We know and understand that you are here to heal your fears, bring forth your talents, and especially we always see the truth of your divine presence; of who you really are. We are here to support your journey.

Through this experience, I felt that Spirit wanted me to know that we are much more than our three-dimensional, intellectual bodies. Our spirit goes far beyond the Earth. This was me being aware of my past life as a Native American Indian. It connected and intersected with what I am experiencing in my life now. I have always carried in my heart gratitude for the forgiveness I received that day from the tribe I belonged to that I had held so dearly in my heart in that life.

What is a trust walk and what makes it so powerful? I learned that you must go into it with an open heart and without expectations. No fears are allowed except the ones you are there to heal. Your spirit guides you to what is blocking you. My block was feeling like I was on the edge of a cliff, and I was guided to take that step of faith. You must have faith in the greater good for yourself. You are unable to see with your Earth eyes so you must go within and see with your spiritual vision. It takes training to move beyond what those on Earth would have you believe. You must trust your spiritual instincts because they become your strength through your journey. You transcend and move out of Earth internally and learn that spirit is your true guiding light within.

The synchronicities that the spiritual world brings when you are open and seeking to know yourself give insights, such as receiving that phone call from Carla asking me to attend and then showing up not knowing what to expect. I was open to receive. That is when synchronicities happen and unexpected healing can occur. That is when your life is blessed with the experiences that elevate you to higher levels, because you become aware that there is more out there than you have known or experienced before. It comes in increments, but over time you can experience things in your life that you could not have ever imagined.

Spiritual journeys are all about knowing who you really are and not about what the third-dimensional world is telling you. This is an enlightening journey to get in touch with your inner spiritual self. I was caught in a world where I did not fit in by "their" standards. I have learned that I am a spiritual being wanting the third-dimensional world to be a better, more loving place.

If you don't feel like you fit into the world, like I did at the time, then be open to letting those synchronicities find you. Sometimes, the feeling of the impossible leads you to know that possibilities exist. You may feel like you don't fit in because nobody understands you. I know that feeling. I had to go beyond my limits of comfort because I could not keep living if I could not find some level of comfort to be myself and be accepted. I did not choose drugs that allowed me to escape what I did not want to face. I had to muster up courage. It was uncomfortable in the beginning, but the outcome was worth it. Many might gravitate to alcohol, drugs, or other addictive behaviors that will not help them find what they are seeking. It will only give them momentary escapes from a world they do not understand or want to live in. Over time, the avoidances of what you need to see and heal will slowly but surely box you in tighter and tighter until you have little room to move.

The trust walk led me into a journey to find myself and who I am. This journey made me aware that this world can be more than three-dimensional. Seek to explore who you really are. "Know thyself" has been an important credo since the times of Greek mythology. Socrates stated, "True wisdom is knowing what you do not know. So, an essential part of knowing yourself must be recognizing the limits of your own wisdom and understanding . . . knowing what you do genuinely know and knowing what you have yet to learn."

Spiritual journeys like the trust walk I participated in are there to assist you to learn more of your spiritual nature. We are truly divine beings who are seeking to find our divinity within and integrate this part of our inner being into our daily lives. This does not happen without healing the wounds that you carry within yourself. All wounds are fear based. The energy of Love is pure, whole, and complete. There is not a breakdown in its existence. Every wound you heal frees fear-based energy to create what would enlighten you. As you progress, you will find that each wound you heal will bring lightness to your body, emotions, and mind. The heaviness of a wound creates doubts, judgments, and uncertainties that limit your expression and what you want to achieve. If you have ever wanted something but no matter how hard you tried, you have been unable to achieve it, then look within for that little culprit that is hiding inside of you. If you are unable to do this on your own, seek out help or ask your spirit to guide you to someone who can help. In the healing comes the rewards of a new, vibrant life.

I have felt the synchronicities that come to us by divine appointment happening many times. You know you have experienced one when you leave with a feeling of contentment and wonder, finding the intersection of the experience at any given moment unplanned.

My experience with synchronicity or divine appointment is that they are pretty much the same. We are spiritually drawn to intersect with an experience that gives value and awareness to our lives.

How many times in your life have you experienced the unexpected that gave you a welcomed new opportunity, meeting another individual who has a soul connection with you, or a new awareness of another dimension of life? These are the mysteries of life at its best! Be open to receiving synchronicities because they will show up when you least expect them.

Healing Love Practice

The Awareness

Discovery of new dimensions of self can reach far beyond this lifetime.

Have you experienced insight into another lifetime?

What insight and awareness enlightened
you to know this was not random?

The Affirmation

I open to receive the divine healing of Love.

CHAPTER 8

Death From a Spiritual Perspective

One of the hardest and most challenging experiences you will have to go through is the death of a parent, especially if you have been close and connected. We appreciate our parents in a different light as an adult than we did in childhood. We gain more understanding of their role as a parent, especially when we have children of our own. Our children give them the coveted gift of being a grandparent. The special bonds that many create with their parents are from a lifetime of love, challenges, and forgiveness. Parents often have a vision of what their children can become because they see potential that, many times, we are unable to see in ourselves. This is a love that is a deep connection because we were created from their love for each other. There is a lifeline to that connection, and when it breaks, we feel a terrible, painful loss.

I had a deep connection with my father throughout my life. I feel I had a much stronger connection to him than my mother. He lived a simpler down-to-earth lifestyle, and I always felt his love for me. My mother, as much as I loved her, had mental challenges that did not break the bond, but made our relationship more challenging. I did not feel as close to her because she was distracted due to her mental illness, but I do know in my heart that she truly loved me.

My father battled skin cancer in his later years. He had every form there was. While he was visiting me in Galveston, I had him go to a dermatologist. After that experience, he was finished with any further treatment. The doctor had done much more extensive removal than I had anticipated. I felt bad that he was miserable afterward. He told me that he was going to treat it himself and would never go back to a skin doctor again.

Years passed, and eventually he had to address the skin cancer on his face. He walked into the Veterans Administration (VA) to have surgery on his face. I was in my last year as a physical therapy student in Galveston. Only days after he had been there, I drove to Dallas to see him. I walked into his room and saw him lying in his hospital bed. He was weak and his voice was faint. I sat down to observe what was happening and his interactions with the medical staff. A nurse came into his room and said, "Mr. Kent, it's time for your pain medicine."

She administered the medication, and before she left, I asked her, "What are you giving my father for pain?"

The nurse responded, "He is getting morphine. That is what we give to all our terminally ill patients."

I responded abruptly, "No one has told me that my father is terminally ill. I want to talk to the doctor!"

The nurse left the room, and it was not long before she came back to tell me she had the doctor on the phone. I walked out of the room and down the hall to take the phone call. I expressed my concerns and asked the doctor what time he would be making rounds the next morning. I wanted to be there to talk to him face-to-face. The rounds were early, at 6:30 a.m., and I arrived earlier than that. I stood up from my chair when I saw the team of doctors arriving at my father's room. One doctor spoke and told me that he changed my father's medication to a non-narcotic pain medicine. I was relieved to hear that. I told the doctor that I was very concerned that my father had walked into the VA hospital and now he could barely sit up, much less walk.

I was suspicious that they were trying to prevent the surgery, and as long as no one was questioning his course of treatment, they declared him terminally ill until I intervened. They told me he was very weak and did not know if he could make it through the surgery. I knew I had to help him get stronger. I came to the hospital every day and acted as his physical therapist. We started slow. I had the staff get a walker for him to use. We started with small distances, just getting him to the bathroom and back to bed. We built strength every day until he was getting stronger because he was no longer on morphine. He was finally walking down the halls and strong enough for the surgery.

That day came, and I went to the hospital very early that morning because I wanted to have some time with him before they came to get him. We were alone and I shared with him everything I wanted him to know, not knowing if I would ever see him alive again. I shared how much I loved him and that I loved that he was my father. I told him how much my life meant to me because he was there. He shared his feelings with me, and I was so grateful for the heartfelt exchange we had. Thankfully, the surgery was successful, and I was relieved that he was still with us.

About a year and a half later, my father developed a cough, what seemed to be a cold. He went to the VA for treatment and they sent him home, telling him he had to "ride it out;" that it was "just a cold." His cough never got better. After several months, my sister and I decided he needed a second opinion from a doctor not part of the VA. The new doctor diagnosed my father with lung cancer and said he had approximately six months to live. He was placed on hospice, and my sister and brother-in-law took him into their home. I called my sister frequently to see how he was doing. I lived out of state and planned to come in for a long weekend to give them a break and an opportunity to go out for an evening while I stayed with my dad.

They brought in a hospital bed for him and a high-backed chair next to his bed for family who came to visit. He was getting weaker and weaker, losing his appetite, and sleeping on and off throughout the day. He had been anxious and restless, and was somewhat unsettled with what was happening. I could see and feel his fear and resistance.

I was alone with my father this evening. It was around dusk, and I was sitting in the chair facing him as he slept. I rested my head back on the chair and closed my eyes. The energy I began to feel was lifting me into a state of consciousness that was a different, lighter energy. This energy that surrounded me took me into a place where I was shown a vision of a ceremony in progress.

My father's body was lying on a slab that was raised off the ground by a pedestal. His eyes were closed, and he appeared to be in a restful state. As I watched, there were Native American Indians dressed in magnificent headdresses and colorful costumes for the ceremony. They were chanting and dancing around my father's body as their arms raised and lowered in a rhythmic fashion to the beat of the drums. The energy from the ceremony gave off an air of preparation, drawing the Great Spirit for blessings, and preparing my father for the transition back into spirit. I watched in awe of what I was witnessing. I was grateful for the experience that brought me the understanding that when a person is close to death, the spiritual world also plays an important role in the transition of life on Earth back to spirit. My father's grandmother was a full-blooded Native American Indian, so I was not surprised to witness a Native American Indian ritual.

The vision faded and I slowly opened my eyes. I looked at my father as his eyes were opening. He looked at me and the first word he said was "rainwater." I never knew what that meant, but what I did see was my father at peace from that moment on. The only meaning that I can take from this is that he was cleansed of his fear of death and his transition back to spirit was at hand.

I packed up the next day to travel back to Hot Springs, where I was living at the time. Saying goodbye to my father and family was difficult, and I wished that I could have stayed. During the drive back, about an hour out of town, my instincts were very strong in telling me I needed to go back. I stopped at a pay phone and called my sister. I told her the feelings I was having and knew I needed to go back as soon as possible. My plans were to go home and request a week off to be with my dad. My director understood my situation and agreed to give me the time off, and by the next day I was on my way back to Dallas.

I arrived and my father was getting weaker each day. He slept more and stopped eating. One day, the hospice nurse came for a visit. We told her what was happening with his pulse getting weaker and respirations shallower. The nurse asked us if we had told our dad that it was okay for him to go. We looked at each other and shook our heads "No." We went up to his room. I took his right hand, and my sister took his left hand. I told dad that it was okay for him to go. I let him know that he would live in our hearts forever and that we loved him very much. My sister spoke her words she wanted to share. We stayed with him, continuing to hold each hand. We watched as his breaths became shallower. With each exhale, we saw that each inhale was weaker and weaker until he exhaled his last time. We waited for the inhale that never came. The hospice nurse helped us through the feelings of loss in that moment, and his passing became a reality.

The hospice nurse asked if my dad had an animal that belonged to him. "Yes, he does," I responded, and told her his dog, Sissy, was in the next room.

She had me retrieve his chihuahua. The nurse instructed me to place her on the bed with my dad. Sissy walked up and down the bed, sniffing and smelling his body. I could feel the grieving that Sissy felt when she realized he was gone. When the funeral home staff arrived to take him, I picked up Sissy and we left the room.

That night, I stayed in my niece's room across the hall from where my dad had been. I was in bed with Sissy, and we were both grieving the loss we felt together, and the connection we had comforted both of us. As I was beginning to relax to go to sleep and my eyes were closed, my father appeared in the room, and I opened my eyes as my energy sensed this. He looked like he did when he was in his thirties. The image he projected was light and lacked the density of a human body. It was a soft white light with a darker color that outlined his body image, but I could clearly see his face. He was smiling and telepathically told me he was okay and that he was happy.

I felt very blessed to have experienced those moments with him in spirit. My heart transformed the grief and loss into a beautiful memory and gift I was given to see him in spirit. I was now at peace with him crossing over. The whole process of this experience gave me new insight into what I had once known death to be, and confirmed my new beliefs that there is no death at all. There is only the transformation of the soul shedding the physical body and returning to the spiritual realm. I also learned that when anyone is close to leaving the Earth, the spiritual side is preparing the soul for the transition, as well. We are developing new insights into death and dying and learning that death is not the end, but a beautiful beginning back into the world of spirit.

As time passed, I continued to have moments of loss from his absence, but my heart remembered how happy he appeared when he came to me after his death. That always brought me a feeling of comfort. He has continued to live in my heart all these years, just like I told him he would before he passed.

Have you experienced something similar? How has the passing of a loved one changed your life? During these times, sensitivities rise because the heart is open. There is no limit of possibilities that can be experienced if your heart and mind are open and connected to the spiritual world. The passing of a parent is especially difficult, because most of the time, if you have been close, there is a strong connection and many experiences and memories that you have collected over a lifetime. If we are lucky, our parents live a long life to have many memories to hold in our hearts.

I feel the greatest challenge in losing a parent is letting go of any attachments we have created through the emotional bonds of love we have for them. The stronger and deeper the emotional bonds that weave through this love, the greater the sense of loss and wondering how life will go on without them. The emotional bonds of their love can continue to live in your spiritual heart as long as you wish, especially when the attachments are released and the love that remains is unconditional.

If you have lost a parent, does it occasionally feel like a part of your heart is empty? Have you felt them close to you after they pass? This happens more frequently than you think. Don't ever think you are imagining it. Through the years, as spirituality is more recognized, it is becoming a more prevalent happening. Cherish whatever you have with them, whether it is before their passing or after.

As I reflect on my father's memories, he lived a brave life. He was a Marine in World War II who was captured and taken as a prisoner of war by the Japanese for three and a half years. He survived and came home to marry and have a family of four children. He experienced the loss of his only son, which challenged him in many ways. He was a survivor throughout his life. I am grateful for the spiritual awareness I gained through his transition back to spirit. I am so grateful to have witnessed his ceremony to prepare him for his return, which gave him the peace to release his fear of death. This awareness was monumental for me.

Helping a parent through their death and dying process takes an enormous amount of love, compassion, and understanding. The selfless act of knowing and understanding the process to help them will also help you. Even though they are now in the spiritual world, the communication can continue. The communication happens through the spiritual heart, especially if there has been a strong connection of love.

Healing Love Practice

The Awareness

The life-death process is a spiritual experience and asks our awareness to understand that life continues after we die.

How can you hold a higher vision of your loved one that is passing that will bless both of you?

What experiences during or after death has let you know that your loved one lives on?

The Affirmation

I am whole in God's Love.

CHAPTER 9

Life Is Eternal

I reflected upon all my experiences with my family and my experiences of loved ones who have left. When I was four years old, my maternal grandmother passed away. I was told, "Your grandmother has gone to be with God."

I really didn't understand what that meant. I sensed that the statement was supposed to be comforting, but as I looked around, what I felt was unfathomable sadness and loss. Within the same year as my grandmother, my aunt—who was the oldest daughter of my grandmother—also died, and I again found myself at another funeral. My mom had lost her two brothers not too many years earlier, during World War II. Being the sensitive child I was, it was impossible to buffer myself from the mounting pain she felt upon losing her closest family members.

In the 1950s, funerals were heavier with sadness and despair than they are today. There was not the Celebration of Life as we look at it now. When I reflect back, that's the feeling I had—the remembrance of a chasm of emotional bleakness that I wasn't sure I could ever return from.

Death—the transformation from physical form on Earth back to our spiritual essence—is difficult to comprehend, to say the least. Letting go of the ones our hearts are so connected to isn't an experience that the mind alone can process. But I tried to! Death and loss held my curiosity as I grew older. I wanted to understand what really happens when we leave our physical body. There had been so much inner healing during the ten years I worked with Carla that gave me a taste of life beyond the body. Through our deep spiritual focus, I began to have a new understanding of "death," perceiving it for the first time as a "passing." This word felt more real and true. For a soul leaving the Earth, shedding the body in the return to Spirit, "passing" into another realm of existence speaks to the continuity of life beyond the physical. I explored many aspects of the death and dying process, including looking at the many ways we "leave" (through illness, accidents, suicide, and more) and how those circumstances impact the people who are left behind.

But even with all this exploration with Carla, eventually a divine restlessness set in. I felt like I was missing something. It was, perhaps, something beyond any intellectual understanding. My spirit yearned for something beyond what I had already learned, and I began to sense that there was something on the horizon. I prayed for more advanced spiritual experiences, whatever they might be, and my prayers were soon answered.

One day, I opened my mail to find an invitation to apply for a seat at Alan Cohen's first Mastery Training. Alan is a renowned inspirational teacher and author of many books, including *The Dragon Doesn't Live Here Anymore*. I did not hesitate to respond. The main portion of the application was an essay about my spiritual journeys, development, and questions about the aspirations I wanted to move toward. I was accepted as one of only twelve people who would be gathering from all over the country. The Mastery Training was held in Maui, Hawaii, where Alan lived at the time. I was overjoyed with this opportunity. This was what my restless spirit had been searching for.

The group arrived in Maui uncertain about what was planned. Alan was taking direction from Spirit when it came to the itinerary for the week. But what we did know was that the experiences were going to be exciting and mystical. The eleven other people I met in the group were incredibly supportive and loving, and we had so much fun together during our training. Our mornings started with yoga and meditation. This was perfect, as it set the tone and intent for the day. Mid-morning, we received spiritually guided teachings from Alan, often having to do with attuning to our own ability to channel inner wisdom and expanding our awareness of universal truths. In the afternoon, we had free time to explore our own interests. The horses really called to my spirit, so I chose to go horseback riding one afternoon. On another day, we went on a boat with the hope of witnessing the beauty of the whales—beings of such magnificent grandeur. They were mesmerizing to behold. As I watched them move out and back into the water, I felt their flow of energy perfectly in harmony with the flow of the Divine. The whales reminded me how my life was when I was in this flow of Life. Nothing was opposing their dance as their enormous bodies glided through the ocean with beauty and grace. In the evenings after dinner, we came together as a group for a recap of our experiences of the day and to share any enlightening moments. These gatherings were one of the best parts of the week for me. With each shared story, I felt more connection and love with each person.

One of the experiences we had, which was a first for me, was an all-night prayer vigil. We were divided into pairs and given a one-hour window of time during the night when we would take turns in front of the altar that was created by our group. My partner Sharon and I gave alternating prayers aloud. As we continued during the hour, our prayers flowed harmoniously together, and we felt an upliftment of spirit within us. The time passed so quickly being in the elevated energy that filled the room. A rabbi, who was part of our group, sat next to the altar all night, bearing witness to our prayers and I am sure offering his own. I was moved by what happened spontaneously as I got into the flow of the prayers—I *knew* that I was speaking directly from my spiritual heart.

By dawn, the energy in the room was buzzing—filled with the power of Spirit embodied by each one of us. We all circled together in the room and offered one more prayer as a group. I will never forget the energy that was present—the dance of love, enlightenment, and grace that I believe each of us could feel. We knew we had co-created the sacred ground we were now standing on. I think that's the kind of realization that changes a person.

Afterward, I was taken aback when the rabbi shared with Sharon and me that the prayers spoken by us were some of the most beautiful he had ever heard. It was confirmation that both she and I had, indeed, been speaking from the heart. A holy man had witnessed it! In a world that prioritizes the power of the mind, it's a deep relief to be guided into prayer by a loving feeling rather than arid ideas about what prayers *should* be.

Not all transformative experiences happen in such exalted ways, as you may well know. Sometimes the most humbling moments are where the greatest gifts are found. At a week-long workshop like the Mastery Training, there are two words that I think most people don't want to hear: *kitchen duties*. So, of course, at the orientation session, we were asked to take turns with kitchen duties. My first uncensored, private reaction was that I had come to the retreat expecting to be served my meals and not involved with clean up or anything to do with food for the week. Honestly, I thought this was beneath me. Ah, the voice of the ego can so easily take on a tone of righteous indignation, can't it? However, the actual *experiences* I had in the kitchen allowed my ego expectations to quickly and completely dissolve. What really happened during our shared "duties" was that I connected with the people on my shifts. We laughed, shared stories, confided some of our deepest dreams and longings, and had a blast. I relaxed, opened, and felt so much love for my apron-wearing kitchen cohorts. Alan had wisely woven this assignment into the fabric of the training, understanding that being of service to others offers some of the greatest leaps forward in our growth. For me, it was a gift that I will always cherish.

Each of the workshop moments I've described so far—little snapshots of a whole panorama of growth and awakening that took place inside that week—were the prelude to something I had been wishing for my whole life, ever since that little girl I used to be was quietly devastated by toxic levels of fear and grief about death. Although I wasn't yet aware of it, the days leading up to the final session of the training were preparing me for a profound release.

The last morning, Alan was leading us through another meditation. At a certain point, I could no longer hear his voice. Instead, I became aware that I was being lifted up by Spirit into an otherworldly place. I understood that my transition from Earth was about to take place, and I began to feel a resistance. In truth, "resistance" is putting it mildly. I was holding on with all my might. I battled letting go and tried to control the situation until I eventually became fatigued.

Just as I gave up the battle, it was as though Spirit removed the veils so I could see clearly. I became acutely aware that what I was resisting was the loss of my Earthly identity, and that my true self was far beyond identity. I saw and felt that who I really am is more than what appears in the physical realm. I fully comprehended the truth of this for each and every one of us on Earth. With this recognition, I felt myself letting go—experiencing the death of the limiting beliefs and perceptions of who I was. I sensed and knew with every fiber of my being that I am one with the Spiritual Universe of Oneness—always and forever. I felt a wholeness that I had never felt in my Earthly life. I was in awe.

It's hard to describe the freedom I felt. There was now nothing within me opposing anything in this experience. There was a pure lightness as I understood that only Love exists. This unexpected gift came as a response to many years of questioning death, mostly out of fear.

There had been many times in my life when I was in so much pain that I was willing to die to know the truth. These were my dark nights of the soul. And suddenly I felt so much compassion for myself and gratitude for having persevered through my many hardships and wounds, seeing that each one brought me closer to my experience that day.

Some aspects of the wonder I found myself in during the meditation are nearly impossible to put into words. The magnitude of oneness—the grandeur of this divine energy—was greater than anything I had ever experienced. Countless times I had tried to imagine it, but it was simply more than what my human self alone could ever hope to embrace. And all of it brought me home to a truth that can heal lifetimes of heartbreak for any one of us:

> *There is no death—not for that which is real and eternal. There is no death for that which breathes life into these miraculous bodies during our time on Earth.*

This felt experience was so *huge* that I wanted to share it with the group, but time did not permit. When the time had come for Alan to close the circle and say goodbye, I understood from Spirit that I was meant to hold this close within my own heart for a time—to integrate and absorb the gift that was given to me before talking about it.

Well, I'm ready to talk about it now! And to *not* share it would be such a missed opportunity, especially since the lessons from that week had given me a new depth of compassion for all of us when it comes to how we perceive death. I feel empathy for the struggle so many of us have in letting go of our Earthly identities. We feel like we are losing ourselves and the lives we have built, along with losing everything we've experienced with our loved ones. But truly, this story of loss is the last illusion of the ego.

I looked back on my father's passing and realized that this was the struggle he had gone through for a period of time. He fought valiantly to hold onto to his identity. After a Native American Indian ritual took place to help him surrender into the arms of the Great Spirit, my father was at peace until he passed several days later. My week on Maui gave me a healing glimpse of this peace—the peace that passeth all understanding.

It's impossible to measure the depth of loss any one of us feels when someone we love dies, and we each process our losses differently. At the more extreme end of grief, some people choose not to feel anymore. Their grief and loss are so severe that they seek escape through drugs, alcohol, overworking, or other kinds of addiction—anything that will numb the pain. And some people give up altogether, finding it next to impossible to function without their loved one. The more attachments we have to the person who leaves, the less we may feel complete without them. That is when healing the wounds of attachment is necessary. Being *bound* to others results in the emotional energetic heaviness that I felt around me as a child. That's the weight that feels inescapable when it's bearing down on us. But it is escapable.

With awareness and love, we can be free of the two-ton bolder of pain. We can raise our spiritual vibration higher than the octave of grief alone. We don't want to bypass grief. We just don't want to stay there too long. The grief of loss is a natural human emotion, but when we dwell in it, and our life becomes lost in sorrow, that is when we are not serving anyone—especially ourselves. Our healing of any loss of a loved one, even a pet, comes when we begin to let the light in. This is the light that comes as grace amid the darkness. Sometimes, the light comes fast and shines big and bright. And sometimes the light comes slowly and faintly. We may overhear ourselves wondering: What insight have I discovered? Grief is healing, wallowing in pain and holding on to the past is not healing. Feeling the one that has passed and holding the memories and love you keep in your heart is what you should try to embrace with their transition. Tears will come with future events, and you feel your loved ones with you, but that is healthy. Live with them in your heart forever without pain.

From the depths of sorrow to the heights of oneness with the divine, I now embrace the totality of this human journey. Through my Mastery Training experience, I remembered something I have always known but had been asleep for a time—that nothing can truly separate us from each other or from our true selves. Yes, there is a human arc that we know as "birth and death," but *life* itself is eternal. Life holds birth and death in its capable arms.

My hope is that your own remembrance of this truth grows stronger with each passing day. In fact, see what happens when you *invite* this knowing to be fully restored.

Healing Love Practice

The Awareness

Death is only a passage from Earth back into the Life of Spirit.

Has your passed loved one let you know they are still with you?

Have you connected with a loved one who is returning to spirit?

The Affirmation

I accept death as a natural part of life without fear.

CHAPTER 10

The Healing Power of Prayer

I questioned whether to write this chapter, because what can I say about prayer that has not already been written? I was guided to do so anyway. What Spirit wants to remind everyone is to ask for what you want and not for what you want to avoid. There is more power with what you want that has not manifested than to be saved from what you don't want that you need to be redeemed from. One is an upliftment and the other is a plea to save you from drowning. Jesus was known for showing and teaching us how to pray. He always looked toward his Father to bring upliftment and support to the people of his era. The messages and prayers were always about raising above what seemed to be pulling one down and instead seeing a vision of what could be achieved. The circumstances were all about what one wanted to be raised toward; seeking a vision that could be seen and could be manifested. Prayer has always been about upliftment, support, and moving toward the greater good.

Prayer has been one of our most coveted gifts given to ask for whatever healing or assistance we need. Prayer requires a belief in something higher than our own limited vision. Prayer offers us a way to reach into a state of humility, Love, and connection. The humility takes us inward, where we release our state of significance and ego importance to bring forth the greater power of God's presence into our energy. Our hearts open to the presence of Love, and experiencing that Presence is enlightening. In this sacred connection, what we ask for will be heard.

Prayer transcends all religions and becomes a sacred journey of the spiritual heart. The spiritual heart has no need for a religion, for it is directly connected to God's Lifeforce. I was raised in Christian churches from Presbyterian to Baptist to Unity. I have experienced value in all of them while I was searching, from the time I was a young child into my adult years, for that connection with God. During those days, God seemed to be outside of me.

I was living in Galveston and hosting one of Carla's Intensives at my home. I had been searching and longing for a direct connection with God. One afternoon during a break, I will always remember the special moment when God became real within me. I was in my bedroom with my best friend Rosalyn. I felt this gentle, loving energy that was opening within me. The feeling was so soft and peaceful. I could not speak as tears gently rolled from my eyes. Another friend came into the room and asked what was wrong. Rosalyn told her that God was now real within me. She was acutely sensitive to what I was experiencing internally. That moment changed my life. I no longer had to search for God outside of myself.

Prayer changed for me that day. I felt a flame of light within me that was very sacred. I humbled myself when I went before this flame, embracing the love and compassion of my being before asking anything. Prayer has a deeper meaning and connection that I am now able to experience. What I understand now is the intent and Love we hold with prayers gives our answers. The answers may not always be what we expect, but the outcome can possibly exceed our expectations.

I have learned that there is a difference between pleading for something in prayer and seeing with a vision that it has already manifested as you ask in prayer. Your vision is seeing the perfect outcome. We pray to ask for healing of others. We pray to ask for help in our careers, as well as for our families and friends. Many times, we pray for ones that we don't know personally, but there is a need for these souls to have food to eat and to help them out of the circumstances of their living environment. There are many circumstances and situations on this Earth that need our prayers.

I wanted to understand about the true process of death, so my prayers were sent up and I let go of them. The prayers were answered as they were ready to unfold. I believe that is why I experienced the Native American Indian ritual just prior to my father's passing. My prayer was answered when my father came to me after he passed to show me that he was very much alive in spirit and that he was happy. My prayer finale was the Mastery Training where I was lifted up from the meditation and experienced crossing over, shedding my physical body, and returning to the spiritual world. These were the blessings and answers I received from prayer. The most important thing after saying any prayer is to let go. The answers will come in divine timing that we have no control over but releasing them allows our experiences to come.

My prayers flowed as I was working to successfully complete physical therapy school. I had to reach deep within myself to find the confidence to complete this. What I overcame were my insecurities of feeling I lacked the intelligence and being good enough, which transcended to having the faith within myself to keep going no matter what and bolstering my inner strength to persevere through whatever came before me. I took it one day at a time, and one semester brought the next. As time moved on, I looked back at what I had accomplished and felt grateful. I realized I had to do the work to overcome my insecurities. God could not magically make them disappear. If He did, I would not have gained all the personal growth that came because I believed in what I wanted to accomplish. I believe that was God's gift to me; that the answer to my prayers was His faith in me to keep reaching deeper within myself.

I have met people who wanted to be saved from their poor decisions and from the depths of what they had created in their lives. I am aware of this because I was one of those people earlier in my life. I always remembered the saying, "Don't dig a hole so deep that it is difficult to find a way out." I dug many deep holes during that portion of my life when I was living without direction. Yes, I went to church, but internally, I felt empty. Everything I seemed to be experiencing was outside of myself. My heart now goes out to these people because you want to help them, but you cannot save them from themselves. They live in a world where they seek a solution outside of themselves or a quick fix. They are unaware that they have created the world they are living in by right of their consciousness. This is when I send prayers to help them find the beauty of their own spirit and discover that they are their own salvation. I had to save myself at one point in my life because I had exhausted every other avenue. For the ones who have not found their way out, I bless their journey and acknowledge their true spirit of who they really are. By doing that, I am acknowledging their divinity of who they are in truth and holding the light for their human soul to awaken within.

I was fortunate to live in a time when prayers were allowed in public schools. We had an overhead speaker that was projected from the principal's office into each classroom within the school. We closed our eyes and bowed our heads as a prayer was said each day. I remember, also, when the schools were no longer able to say prayers like many of us were able to experience until I was twelve years old. In 1962, the U.S. Supreme Court banned school-sponsored prayer in public schools. In 1963, The Supreme Court outlawed mandatory Bible study courses in schools, but ruled that schools may teach objectively about religion, as opposed to teaching religious indoctrination. Then, in 1980, the Supreme Court removed The Ten Commandments from public schools. The Supreme Court has never banned students from praying voluntarily and privately on their own, provided there was no state intervention. Students must simply do so without the guidance or coercion of school authorities. For a student like me, in those days it was confusing to understand why these things were being mandated. Many people were taken aback by the changes being made in public schools, but prayer continued anyway, the only difference was that we did not have a school-led prayer in the mornings.

As prayer continues to give us strength, comfort, and hope, we have an avenue to connect our inner spirit with the grace of God. Our hearts continue to open to that connection where we can be heard and connect to the ultimate power that created us. We have searched so many thousands of years for the truth of our being. The energy is rising on Earth as a result of the growing number of people searching spiritually. As the consciousness of our spiritual nature rises with more people seeking, our connection to the spiritual world grows more easily assessable. More than religion, we are also searching for the divine connection of our spirit to the spiritual world that is so close, such as through our spiritual guides and angels who help to guide our paths. As we become aware of them and connect with them, our lives are enriched because we can open channels within ourselves to hear and feel them. I have been aware and connected to my spiritual guides since their presence became known to me in the early 1980s. They are very real and know your destiny and why you came here. They are the ones who help you in your darkest moments. They are truly a God source that is supportive of your higher good.

One of the things I realized once I crossed over into the spiritual world was that there is no separation of God's source of Love. Everything is connected in an energy of Love. Here on the Earth, where each of us has a body that is separate from the other bodies on the planet, we have the illusion that we are indeed separate beings. In the spiritual world, there is a connection of oneness to the source, which is God. As past lives have been revealed to me from spiritual visions, I understand the multidimensional intersections of each particular life and how it relates to my life now. Not everyone may experience this, but peering into those lives has helped me in the healing of the wounds that were there.

The more we open to possibilities in our lives, we open our vision to see into realms beyond the limitations of Earth, with prayer many times helping us to achieve this. That is how some of the greatest inventors of our time created what we have today. Think of where our own lives can go if we open ourselves to the possibilities of our life and what we can do with it. I am relieved that there is so much more out there yet to be discovered and we are not limited to a third-dimensional world that can many times limit what we can see, hear, or experience. Prayer has transcended for me over the years from limiting my prayers from a three-dimensional world view to the more universal, spiritual realm. I am so grateful for my sensitivity that has allowed me to explore beyond a limiting Earth mentality. The spiritual insights I have gained from these adventures have broadened my scope of God, the healing that has opened doors, and the upliftment these journeys have given me. My prayers now embrace the universal presence of a living, loving God.

Prayer has been very much a part of my life from the beginning. I did have to pray and project beyond what I wanted for the fullness of my true self to come to life. My journey in life has progressed me to a place where I feel humbled by it. I feel blessed that I have reached this point in my life, which my soul and my spiritual friends have guided me to achieve. Years ago, I always had a sense that I would write a book. I did not know what it would be, but now I know that my life was designed to discover myself, and in that discovery to help others in the process of their own self-discovery.

If you have not yet reached that level, you are not alone. I am seventy-three years old and every time I thought I had achieved what I came to Earth to do, I discovered more. We are here to learn and grow on this Earth. It is a place where you can decide your ending point if you choose. The universe is infinite and is designed for us to keep growing with our hearts' desires. The grace that God has given me has allowed me to give you a glimpse of what is awaiting you if you work on your own growth in this human form. Life is not always easy, but it is easy when it comes to the growth of your own soul. Your life is worth the journey to live and move beyond the limitations of Earth to find the spirit of who you truly are.

Prayers, I have come to understand, are for our own salvation. God is full and complete in Love. As we pray for what we want and are searching for within ourselves, the road ahead brings special blessings to keep guiding and moving us forward into our destiny and why we are here.

May the roads we travel be blessed with our human growth and elevation to clearly see a path of love and enlightenment on our journey. This is my prayer for every human soul.

Healing Love Practice

The Awareness

We affirm our prayers through our love and connection with God.

Are your prayers asking for spiritual healing
or salvation from your fears?

What enlightenment can I bring through
my prayers for others and myself?

The Affirmation

I am whole in God's Love in whatever I ask in prayer.

CHAPTER 11

The Healing Power of Surrender

Forgiveness may be the most powerful form of surrender that dissolves the unforgivable into the forgivable by bringing love and understanding into the equation. There is a two-part situation to review in healing any disconnections: your perception and the other person's perception. What creates misunderstanding, hurt feelings, or separation from one another is how you define its meaning. The core of each party's belief system is the base through which all harmony or disharmony arises. It is by right of your own consciousness from your belief system that sets all of this in motion.

In my lifetime, I have surrendered to many things, but not without the struggle of holding on to what was not serving me and not understanding the process that was before me. Healing emotional wounds has been a struggle many times because I did not understand the process of transforming energy from the fear that created the wound in the first place into free energy that I could use to create what serves me and allow what I wanted to manifest. This process was a journey throughout my life to undo what I held on to that was not serving my spirit or my higher good. Many times this block or wound would prevent what I truly wanted to find its way to me. The ego can create fear and doubt better than anything I know. I fell into the trap of my ego many times until higher spiritual education and enlightenment entered my life, and then it became less of a struggle, but it definitely helped me through many obstacles.

Surrender, I have come to understand, is recognizing when I am supporting fear-based energy and bringing a higher truth to the situation that allows me to make a choice when I see the reality of the fear. Fear restricts and love expands. When I surrender to fear when it surfaces, and replace it with an energy that supports and expands my energy, then I can release what is false (fear) and embrace a concept of Love energy to replace it. I am able to surrender once I understand the situation that created it, understand my circumstances at the time to adopt it as my own, and then forgive the situation and circumstances surrounding it. Forgiveness and understanding are the Love energy that transforms fear back into Love.

The awareness and enlightenment that come with the knowledge of surrender and why we are being asked to do this is the key to our inner growth from anything that limits us. This is what I came to understand through my resistance and struggles in my own life. When I encounter resistance, I know I am facing a fear that I created by "right of my own consciousness," which I learned through my teachings from Carla.

I never knew that surrender carried so much power until I signed up for Michael Singer's course, "Living from A Place of Surrender," which came from his book *The Untethered Soul*. I went through his course and read his book and was amazed and humbled from the teachings of both. A new door of awareness opened for me spiritually, as well as healing many issues from the past.

The whole experience of his course was a profound wealth of knowledge and awareness about life on Earth and how we interpret, or rather misinterpret, our daily interactions with the experiences that we are offered every day. I realized that surrender could be experienced in two different ways. I have the opportunity to release easily with my awareness of it, or I can choose to resist surrender until I am taken down by it. By that, I mean that I waste so much energy of my true inner enlightened self if I resist an energy that is attempting to set me free from the negative forces of my own consciousness that I created.

In the past, I was conditioned to believe that surrender is a form of weakness or defeat. Surrender has been defined as and believed to be defeat, and defeat results in a weaker person or group who has been overpowered. The wars through history were about conquering and being victorious over the opponent. Once the opponent surrendered, they were defined as the weaker of the two at battle. They had been defeated and they surrendered. My old conditioning caused me to resist and fight for what my inner existence of fear-based experiences presented. The new concept I have come to know spiritually is that surrender is there to see my old experiences in a different, more enlightened way.

What Michael Singer brought me was a higher elevation of my consciousness that I lacked. What this new insight taught me was to step back and observe how I truly interacted with my world. This was a breakthrough moment for me spiritually. When my awareness was sharpened by his teachings, I could see that what seemed to be the most mundane of my life interactions turned out to be the most important ones of my life. I could finally see that I had not recognized the depth of consciousness my life was reacting to.

I was in this new place of realization when I was traveling for a celebration retreat that the new Holistic Life Coaches created for the completion of our training that was being held in Aspen, Colorado. We had all stayed connected through emails and texts. Most of us had started reading *The Untethered Soul*, which I had suggested as the first book for our group's new book club. On the flight to Colorado, I was conscious of choosing to surrender to our plane's delayed departure. I looked around to observe how people were reacting to this delay, remaining distant to energies stirring and different emotions making their presence known. I could hear comments from passengers complaining and allowing the delay to shift their mood. I was aware that I could be drawn into these unfriendly emotional reactions to the flight delay, or I could just surrender to the experience, and that is what I chose to do. This required me to remain in my state of acceptance of the situation and not place any meaning to it. Even though I missed the evening dinner with the group, I accepted my delay and flowed with the energy that was my experience of a delayed plane. Once I arrived, I had to get transportation from Denver to Arvada, where I was to meet up with the coach that would give me a ride to Golden, where I was staying.

I had collected my bags at the Denver airport and used my Uber app to get a driver. I was surprised by how little time it took for the driver to show up. This Uber experience felt like the Universe was sending a driver to help me safely arrive to my destination. As we talked, he told me that he did not usually work for Uber on the day that I arrived. He told me that he decided to take one ride that evening, and that ride happened to be me. He was experienced with the area, and even though we came upon a traffic jam on the freeway, he got off and used the back roads to get me to Arvada. Christine, my ride from Arvada to Golden, texted me as we got closer and told me she would turn on her headlights so that we could spot her easily. The driver was very grateful, as we were entering a neighborhood that was unfamiliar and too dark to see where to drop me off. I felt that Spirit was guiding all of this, especially when such synchronicity was happening. The surrender on the plane earlier, I felt, opened the door for the synchronicity of events to follow. We met Christine easily and then I was on my way to Golden.

Our retreat was uplifting on many levels. We all enjoyed the time together and the gifts and talents we all shared with each other, such as tarot and reiki. Aspen was beautiful, with majestic mountains surrounding us. We enjoyed hiking the trails with the water flowing rapidly to our left as we ascended the trail. There were parts of the trail that were very steep and challenging for me at my age. At one point on the trail, I came upon a very steep, rugged path. As I looked up at the trail facing me, my first thought was that it was too difficult for me to attempt and to let the others go on and I would meet up with them later. I stepped back from the picture I was projecting in my mind that I could not do it. The voice inside me reminded me of something I learned from Tony Robbins: "When you can't, then you must!"

That was all it took for me to move forward and continue up the trail. I made it to the top of that steep part of the trail and felt accomplished when I was able to do it successfully.

After a meaningful and enlightening four days of reuniting with all the coaches, the time had come to return home. Christine and I drove from Aspen back to Golden, and the rich conversations we shared created a strong connection between us and a deeper understanding of each other's lives. Time transcended the drive back as we shared our experiences that were meaningful and inspirational to both of us. We were back in Golden as if very little time had passed.

The next morning, Christine drove me to the airport as my flight was leaving from Denver. We had a traffic delay on the way, and I got to the airport around 10 a.m., with my flight leaving at 10:40 a.m. I tried to check my bag, but the lady at the counter said they cut off checking bags forty-five minutes before the flight departs. She asked me if I wanted her to put me on a later flight, and I had to make a decision. I said, "No." She told me to go to the tunnel and pointed in the opposite direction of the sign that said, "To All Gates." I followed and trusted what she said.

I arrived at the security checkpoint with two bags, and the TSA pre-check lane was closed. After I had cleared the body scanner, they sent me back to the other side to take my computers out and run them through. I had my phone and purse to go through again and had to return to the body scanner. They proceeded to physically check the bag I was going to check and took out my facial cleanser (not cheap) and my handmade soap (no big deal), and said I had to leave these if I wanted to board the plane. I released them to the universe and went on my way.

On the way to the gate, now having two bags instead of one, I was faced with going down a flight of escalators to get to the gate. I attempted it, but realized I couldn't do it safely. I had to find someone to help me locate the elevator. As soon as I was down on the level to reach my gate, I realized that my cell phone was missing. I had another decision to make. I had to let my cell phone go because I did not have time to retrace my steps.

Suddenly I realized, as I was racing to the gate, that my boarding pass was on my phone (it was a mobile pass). I just thought I had to get to the gate and then I would figure out what to do. The last people were boarding the plane when I arrived. I went to the counter and asked the lady if she could print me a paper boarding pass due to the loss of my phone. She did and checked in my larger bag with a priority sticker to load in the cargo area with other checked bags. I made it on the plane and settled in. We left the gate and the plane stopped and announced we were waiting on the DFW airport to clear due to weather. We were delayed for an hour.

This was a trial and tribulation of my spiritual journey. I took a nice deep breath and reflected on the meaning of all that I was experiencing. I was being called to let go of attachments and expectations. I knew everything I lost was replaceable. I did not resist the loss and graciously released it all to the universe.

My small carry-on bag was up in the overhead storage area, and I wanted to get my book (*The Untethered Soul*) so I could read it while we were waiting to take off, which the flight attendant helped me do. Of course, the chapter I was reading on the plane was all about what I was experiencing: letting go of attachments and things that we attach meaning to. I finished the book and felt my flight journey to and from Colorado had been an opportunity to practice and put into action what I was taught throughout the book.

I landed in Dallas and got off the plane. I went to the bathroom, and while there I took a moment to put my book in my carry-on bag and saw my phone that I thought I had lost in the front pouch. I was shocked! I retrieved my luggage and headed to the valet. At that point, I realized that my favorite North Face coat was missing. My ticket stub to retrieve my car was in that jacket. The man said that he needed that stub. I showed him the text they sent me now that I had my phone. He said that I was at the wrong valet. He pointed to where I needed to go, to a man standing across the street with a red shirt. I retrieved my car, and even though I did not get the detail job on my car that had been promised, they did do a great job of washing my car inside and out while I was gone. Does anyone else's life sound like this? I know there are worse horror stories about flying, but my experience was bringing so many new awarenesses and opportunities to make different choices.

The reason I wanted to share my airline journey is that you cannot read this book without truly being tested during the process to see if you learn what the author is teaching. That was the day when I realized that I was aware of a higher level of spiritual understanding and inner strength. There was no resistance with the loss and the challenges. I surrendered and let it pass through me. The feeling that I took with me from that experience was what a beautiful spiritual journey surrendering to chaos and loss was.

On my drive home, I was feeling the presence of Love embracing my whole being, and everything I was viewing out of my car window was reflecting a state of peacefulness. My gratitude was overflowing for this experience of surrender and release. Empowerment filled my emotions as I released what I had no control over and realized how much I gave to my spirit in letting go of any resistance. I realized that we can attempt to oppose what we are facing in any experience that we encounter, but in the letting go of the material possessions or expectations that we have assigned excessive value to is a lesson of surrendering to a higher power that lives within—your spirit and Love.

Surrender is, indeed, a higher power of self-realization; your gift and love to yourself. Whatever you face that opposes you is a clue to re-evaluate how you are perceiving the experience. My situation during my travel to Colorado was only the training ground to lead me to the greatest surrender of all: the surrender of the ego. The ego wants you to believe that you have your own special identity other than your spirit. Your true and only identity, as your practice of surrender grows, is your spirit and all it embraces with the oneness of God.

Healing Love Practice

The Awareness

***Every experience in life invites your
response outside of human conditioning.***

Are you aware and accepting of the circumstances you are in,
or do you get entrapped with human conditioning?

What power did you give to a situation that
created an unexpected outcome of peace?

The Affirmation

I become aware of circumstances that are
out of my power to change and accept them.

CHAPTER 12

The Dark Night of the Soul

There are many misconceptions and myths about "the dark night of the soul." It carries a distinct sense of "the dark side" or evil. Actually, it is the most beautiful spiritual experience on the other side but is also the most challenging because you have to have the courage and trust in Spirit to move through. What you feel is death at your doorstep and an ending to life as you know it. Some feelings come to you that are discomforting, and you begin to see pictures in your mind of what the situation could be bringing. It builds in your imagination, and it feels very real, but these pictures are in the future you are about to enter; an experience of life you are moving toward but haven't yet reached. You may question, "What is this about?"

Visions of possible harm lurk in your thoughts, and this energy attempts to seek your withdrawal from it. The energy of fear would be delighted for you to move away. What did this experience feel like for me? I was feeling uncomfortable with this energy of doom and destruction surrounding me. Although I felt this presence, I acknowledged it and then attuned spiritually to guide me to understand what was happening. I stayed focused on my spiritual guidance to trust this energy. I was entering a darkness that spirit was guiding me through. I entered this with a belief and trust that whatever might happen, I was spiritually protected.

This experience came when I was scheduled for a retreat in Maui, Hawaii, in 1995. I was living in Arkansas and working as a contract home health physical therapist. I would travel through two counties each day to evaluate and treat patients in their homes. Living in the mountains in northern Arkansas, driving to patients' homes gave me time to connect with nature as I drove from one house to the next. Most of the patients were at least ten miles apart, but I did not mind because this gave me time to absorb the beautiful scenery with the tall trees and mountains that stretched out for miles in the distance. I loved the times of reflection, and that nature always uplifted me spiritually as I was absorbing the beauty from my car windows.

I was in a relationship with a man I had met through a friend living in Hot Springs, Arkansas. He reminded me of my father, and that may be the reason I was so attracted to him in the beginning. My father had passed away less than a year prior to my meeting Paul. The relationship between us was not going well in that I realized I was more attached to him than he was to me. We really had little in common, but I loved the potential I could see in him, and I was sure he would move toward that. As time moved on, I began to see glimpses of visions with doubts concerning my relationship. I was unsettled with my feelings of discomfort, and one day, a spiritual retreat presented itself. I immediately knew that I was being guided to Maui for a reason, but I didn't know why. The excitement and anticipation I felt was difficult to share with Paul, because he would not have understood.

I was with a man who had no conscious spiritual connection, and there was not a way I could share with him what I was experiencing that he could comprehend. I could feel whenever I was guided spiritually toward a journey of importance, so I did not hesitate to respond. The spiritual workshop was set, and I registered to go, but then I began experiencing doubts. I did not understand these feelings of apprehension, as I was very excited about going. I had dreams and doubts in my mind telling me not to go. I have learned, on the other side, this was my ego trying to create fear within me because of the enlightenment I would experience on this trip.

The day before I was leaving, I was driving toward Izard County to make a house call to my last patient of the day. Admiring the beauty from my car windows, I was enjoying the mountains with the winding roads and the tall trees that lined the small two-lane highway. In my joy and appreciation of what I was seeing, I felt an energy flowing through me, making me aware that the environment I was absorbing and taking in was for the last time. I was taken aback by this thought, as the experience was surreal. *How would I be viewing my world having the awareness and knowing this would be the last time I would experience it?* I felt humbled by the reflection of nature giving me visual examples of its gentle power. As I continued, the appreciation elevated with the beauty that surrounded me, and I took it all in. The energy filling my being was a gentle acceptance of what was happening. If this was my last time to absorb the beauty of this particular nature, I wanted to fully absorb what I was seeing and create memories to take with me.

That night as I was going to sleep, a frightening vision came to me. I was flying to Los Angeles the next day and staying overnight at a hotel and then flying to Maui the following morning. The vision I saw was of myself in the courtyard of the hotel in Los Angeles going to my room at night, and a man was following me. The large man that could overpower me with his strength began to attack me, and I knew he was there to kill me. I was so afraid and ended the vision as soon as the attack started and knew his intent. There was no way I could defend myself, and I did not understand why I was seeing this. As I realized later, the ego will give you whatever it can to keep you from losing its power over you. I went ahead with my plans even though there was fear surrounding me in an attempt to keep me from going.

I arrived in Los Angeles, and during the flight there I had been thinking of my experience with the vision the night before. I prayed for my safety and continued to the hotel. It was dark and there was a courtyard, just like in my vision. Instead of being attacked, I felt an armor of love and safety protecting me. I arrived at my room without incident and all was peaceful. I realized that fear could project whatever power it has to prevent you from moving toward a higher elevation of self if it can instill enough fear to hold you back.

I arrived in Maui the next day. I was in a place that my spirit had longed to be, with like-minded people seeking their own identity in a spiritual world. I enjoyed the whole experience of being spiritually free to live each day being accepted and appreciated for who I was. I gave the same love and acceptance to the others who were there. At the time, I had long straight hair that fell just below my waist. One day, with my hair wet, I divided my hair and made two braids. I wore it like this throughout the day as we hiked through the trails on Maui. By the end of the day, we went back to our condo and prepared for our Hawaiian dance lessons on the beach.

As I took out the braids, my hair flowed with gentle waves down my back. I dressed in a soft Hawaiian gown, and the darkness of my skin that had browned from the sun during the trip made me look native to the island. I wore a halo of small flowers on my head that gave me the final touch to complete my Hawaiian look. I felt authentically ready for the dance. My spirit was alive and celebrating the joy of the moment. Our group arrived for our private dance lessons. What I learned from this experience is the beauty of every purposeful movement we were taught that moved in perfect harmony with the words. The instructor translated what the words meant as we went along. It moved my spirit as I was flowing with my body to the sound and meaning of the music and the dance. This was a spiritual dance of Love and a celebration of life.

The retreat came to an end, and I enjoyed the uplifting experience and the people I had met. As I headed home, I was experiencing a deeper level of appreciation of Love enveloping me. I arrived home and my environment had changed drastically. I saw clearly how the environment that I had been living in had totally transformed. I realized the man I thought I loved did not love me at all. He was not supportive of my growth and became jealous of the life I was moving toward. I realized I was sent on this spiritual journey to know that the environment I was living in was not supporting my spirit. I saw it so vividly when I returned from Maui.

I reflected on the experience of being drawn to Paul because he reminded me so much of my father, who had passed a year earlier. I realized that it was not love for him, but my father, that made me want to make the relationship work. I awakened to the clarity of the toxic relationship that I was in. I was the giver and he was the taker, and by being together we were not serving ourselves, much less each other.

The energy shifts with the highs of spirit and lows of fear/ego that are the creators of the dark night of the soul. It is much like the collisions of two different weather systems that come together and manifest a heavy storm with rain, lightning, and thunder. If you go into the dark night of the soul, your fear will present itself hoping you will be afraid enough to stay paralyzed in that fear you created. This fear wants to live, and you have given it life, just as I did. The truth of the dark night of the soul is about transformation out of fear and the realization that what you created no longer serves you. You dissolve the false sense of being that is not true for you anymore. The dark night of the soul is laying to rest what has haunted you from your fear. Fear is not real; it is only the illusions of your imagination and your psyche. Those ghosts that have been living inside of you are a creation of your own making. The best question to ask at this point is, "What do you want to serve, your spirit or your ego?"

That is the bottom line. Where will you place your focus, and what will you give your energy to? That is the key.

Have you ever wanted to give up on your life, but in the back of your mind you really didn't? Our lives are not perfect for a reason. We are always facing challenges so that we ask ourselves where we want to go. We always have a choice, and it may appear to be easier to give up, but is that what you really want? On Earth, you must have a will stronger than what society tells you to do. You have to reach higher into a reality that many people will not understand, but you do it anyway. There is something within you that has a desire for more of your true self than what you have experienced.

I left the relationship and moved on. What I realized from this experience of the dark night of the soul is that I had lowered my standards at a time after my father's death and attempted to move on with my life without fully healing from my father's loss. My spirit needed this journey to release me from the past and to move me forward. I am grateful for this life experience because it allowed me to grow in the way I did. I cannot hold anything but love for the ones in my life at that time, knowing they were only playing a part for me in my healing.

Sometimes the characters or people that you meet come into your life to play out a part. I see it much like a play. There are roles that each person portrays, some supportive and some taking advantage of your heart and sensitivity. Depending on the situation, sometimes forgiveness is difficult at the time, but made easier as you come to a higher spiritual awareness later. I like to see at it as these people were commissioned by Spirit to play out their roles to help in the healing of my inner wounds. As in my case, being in the relationship allowed me to understand that I needed to let go of the attachment with my father. I also needed to affirm that I am loveable and deserve someone who can love me in a supportive way.

Most of us have experienced relationships that seem to be wonderful in the beginning, but some unexpected challenges came out over time. That is not to say that lasting relationships of love do not have their ups and downs, because they do. The partners in a relationship not only have a deep connection, but also have a foundation of love with perseverance to move beyond the wounds to stay connected in love.

The dark night of the soul is up for many interpretations, but I wanted to give my experience and what I have defined it to mean for me. Whatever you want to call it, this experience is a transition to a higher level within yourself. Because it comes from a deep level within, the whole journey is about healing, and in the healing comes an openness that clears the energy to witness an awareness within yourself; a feeling of breathing in a lighter substance that vibrates throughout your whole being.

We are truly blessed to have the opportunity to witness and embrace a higher good every time we are bold enough to take that sacred step toward the journey and awareness that we came here to achieve. If there is a lesson for the dark night of the soul, it is to know that you have an inner shield of Love on your side that is protecting you as you move toward the enlightenment of your soul that you so deserve to feel and experience.

Healing Love Practice

The Awareness

Love and fear play out their parts to serve the receiver.

Reflect back on your darkest hours
and who came into your life to help.

What are the fears in your life that want
to surface that you are ready to release?

The Affirmation

I release my fears to receive Love.

CHAPTER 13

The Magic of the Inner Child

Truth and innocence are the first words that come to mind when I think about the inner child, along with imagination and creativity adding to those beautiful qualities. We are drawn to babies and toddlers especially because we can witness the innocence of their spirit by observing the world through their eyes. They are curious by nature and intrigued with discovery. At this point, they are experiencing their true spirit being inside a human body that is growing and learning. Their fascination with the smallest discoveries makes them excited, and we experience that joy with them. The inner child has a vivid imagination and may create playful friends that no one else can see except for them, for their minds are open to spirit and spirit responds in a playful way. They have not yet been taught that these imaginary friends do not exist. But do they?

I have come to believe the inner child is the magic and creative flow of energy with which we can create our world when we are truly connected. Each person has an inner child that dwells within their spirit and is felt with the sensitivity of the spiritual heart. This child lives in the imagination and creativity that gives wonder and magic to our lives. The innocence of the child sees no boundaries or restrictions. The child looks at the world with an open canvas to create the dreams of the dreamer. Full of love and acceptance, the innocence of the child embraces the magic that is seen when unexpected miracles happen. I believe that everyone's inner child is a magical part of their spirit.

I lost sight of my inner child for a while as I grew older. The fading of that innocence that I once knew was replaced with the influences of the outside world. I learned about fear and discord from my parents, initially, who argued many nights as I laid in bed trying to go to sleep. The tension of their disharmony created uncertainty for me, and the reality I created in my mindset was a scary, non-supportive place. This became more real than the creativity and playfulness of my inner child. What I adopted in my life through what I was experiencing was loss of control and lack of trust in myself to withstand the outer world I was encountering. As each year passed, I kept piling on a big mound of unhealed wounds. Even when I was facing this, there were friends and others whom I would connect with to temporarily help me out of this fear. Life gives you a chance to come in and out, but you always have to go back to face what you have taken on as your life lessons. The internal wounds weighed me down emotionally.

As my inner child began to visit me again after much spiritual growth and healing many wounds from the past, I was inspired to create healing rooms. That was when I had a clinic for physical therapy, but I was doing more healing/bodywork with the clairvoyant energy that had opened within me. The feeling of creativity flowing through me again uplifted my spirit and made me happy.

One of the things I did creatively was enhance the rooms I worked in to give peaceful and supporting energy where I did sessions for individuals. I painted the room a specific color and the décor I used created a theme. My favorite room that people enjoyed most was my "Native American" room. The color on the walls was a light dusty rose. There were Native American hangings on the wall such as a dream catcher, my sacred arrow bundle hanging below a picture that a friend painted and gave to me of "man ascending becoming angel," and wall tapestries. The colors and wall hangings gave the feeling of safety, support, and love.

One day, I had an idea to create an Egyptian room. This room was very different when I finished. The color on the walls was a deep indigo blue with a touch of teal woven deeply within the color that made it glisten when the light was on it. There were Egyptian decorations on the walls, and of course a sculpture of the head of King Tut that sat on the shelf that finished it off. This room gave off an air of mysticism. If you were comfortable with a mystical surrounding, you loved the room. If not, as many people were, they did not want their session in that room. These rooms were very special to me, as I enjoyed creatively bringing a room to life, so to speak.

My friend John came to have a session and we used the Egyptian room. I had no idea when we began the session what the result would be. I said my prayer as usual, but then I was led inside his energy through his heart chakra. I noticed that I held a light that I carried in my right hand. As I was led deeper and deeper, I began to travel through a ghost town. This was an attempt to scare me to make me go back. I heard, "Do not go further."

Past the ghost town some monsters tried to scare me away. I was aware that the light I was holding was protecting me, and I kept going. I kept going down this energy funnel until I finally reached a closed door. I stopped for a moment and asked Spirit for direction. I was asked to open the door, and I did. There in the closet was a little boy. He looked up at me and I could tell he was frightened. I spoke telepathically to him, and he saw the light of my spirit. Love from my spiritual being was radiating to him so that he knew he was safe. I asked if he would come with me and said that I would protect him. His face changed into a smile that glowed, and he held up his hand. I helped him stand and he came with me. Our energies went upward and funneled through the energy and depth of John's heart. I came back into my body, and I immediately felt John's heart beating with the life of his inner child. I asked John if he could feel the strong heartbeat that I was feeling. He agreed that he could. That was the first and only time I experienced rescuing an inner child that had been buried deeply within my friend to protect this child from the traumatic childhood that he experienced. I understood that John was now very spiritual, and his inner child would be safe.

Many years later, I would have my own experience with my inner child. I woke up one morning and my neck was very stiff and painful to the point that I could not turn my head in any direction. I had not slept on my neck or head wrong during the night. It felt like a huge ball of energy was stuck in my neck. The restriction and pain were so severe that I went to my doctor that day. There was nothing they could do except give me a steroid pack and a muscle relaxer. I never took what was prescribed. Instead, I wanted to try something milder and took Aleve. Each day I began to feel my neck becoming more flexible, and as it did, there was old, uncomfortable energy leaving my body. All I could do is surrender to it, and within a week my neck was back to normal. I felt this lighter energy throughout my body.

These energy shifts that I was going through came from seeking more of my connection with my spiritual nature. I wanted more in life that was uplifting, loving, and embracing of a higher frequency in my being. During the first half of the year, I had been watching Lee Harris and his guides in *Transmissions 2021* with the first module being "Remember Your Magic." I have followed Lee's monthly energy tune-up, as well. All the teachers that had come to me came because I was seeking. Spirit knows your journey and will bring the right teachers when you are ready. Remembering my magic was enlightenment and beauty to my soul.

My birthday party was coming up, and since my birthday is in July, we always made it a pool party. I was in the pool when my niece came over with her children. I had not seen them in weeks, and I was amazed at how the girls had grown. I looked at Susan, my great niece, stepping onto the deck of the pool. I saw this radiating light from her being. It was as if life was creating a slow-motion experience of this observation. She had this gentle smile and had her eyes fixated on me, which was out of character for her. There was unconditional love radiating from her to me. Her face and body were glowing and projecting an angelic golden light energy. The love and acceptance radiating from her was giving me a feeling of value and worth. Spirit had given me my greatest birthday gift, to see and experience my inner child through my great niece. I knew that I was experiencing her in another dimension. I do not know which, but I do know that what I was looking at was not of the third dimension.

What was being given to me by spirit was that my inner child was showing me what she looked like using Susan's body to let me see her presence. She continued the gentle smile and extended her arms out to me. I was in awe of the beautiful child standing before me. I had a small beach ball in my hands. She was waiting for me to throw her the ball. We played catch back and forth, and she kept smiling when she missed my bad throws. She was so radiant that I thought I was seeing an angel before me. Our games progressed to each of us having a ball and we would throw our balls to each other at the same time to hopefully make the catch. That was fun for a time and then we progressed further. There was a sitting area underneath an enclosed dome that was built with a rock foundation. There was a waterfall that came over the flat rooftop dome. She climbed the rock archway where the waterfall came down. Our game now became that she would jump, and I would throw the ball to her before her upper body hit the water. We did this over and over, perfecting our timing and technique. As she missed and swam toward me, I would ask her what she thought I could do to improve my timing to help her catch the ball. She was very excited that I asked. She offered what she thought would help. I realized that we were working together as a spiritual team to support one another. We did not focus on what was not happening, but on what we could do to improve our skills and timing. A true divine team effort.

As I look back, I can see that the experience that day was a very rare gift. I noticed that her mother was observing everything happening as she lay at the poolside sunbathing and keeping an eye out for her children. She noticed how engaged Susan and I were but did not know our true spiritual interaction. Activities of family members were happening in the pool all around us, and yet we were in a space in time where the world we were experiencing was separate from all of the activities around us. And as time would have it, the magic slowly drifted away. Our beautiful spiritual connection was gone as we entered back into the third-dimensional world. We began connecting with everyone else at the party and continued to have fun. Being given the gift of experiencing my inner child through my great-niece was very sacred. Susan normally is shy and and reserved, just like I was as a child. She normally plays with her sisters and does not give me one-on-one time like I experienced. That day, with the Light of Spirit shining through her, she radiated a light and essence I had never experienced before. When it was finished, she became her normal Susan-self and played with others.

I hold that memory with deep appreciation in my heart, and I am thankful to Spirit for this gift. To witness, interact, and play with my inner child made my birthday. I realized how very special it was and the meaningful importance of the inner child. My inner child is alive and well within me, helping me create from what I have built spiritually within me and leaving behind a past that I had to overcome and have grown beyond. My inner child is very important and sacred to me because of the spiritual aspect within her of creative ideas, visions of possibilities, and a reclaimed playfulness that my life truly wanted and needed. We all have one. When you search for the spirit within you and you awaken to that, your inner child lives and dwells within that sacred place of your spirit. Your life will never be the same once this inner child is unleashed within your new world of spiritual truth.

With my awareness that my inner child is alive and well within me,

I must make sure that she is nurtured. She is sacred to me now that I have rediscovered her value and importance in my life. Everything I want to create with her magic and creativity helps me move toward manifesting the love, truth, and awareness of the spirit within me. Whenever you feel your creative genius at work, your inner child is there. Whenever you feel your imagination exploding with new ideas and direction for your life, your inner child is actively involved. When we can connect and partner with our inner child, we can move mountains and can transform the impossible into possibilities that manifest in our lives.

Healing Love Practice

The Awareness:

*The inner child lives within and awakens
the possibilities of creativity and adventure.*

When have you experienced the playfulness
of your inner child as an adult?

How has your inner child brought color
to your black and white experiences?

The Affirmation

My inner child is a reminder of my innocence and creative nature.

CHAPTER 14

The Death I Never Saw Coming

It was October 9, 2021. I received a call at work from my youngest son, Billy. He said, "Mom you need to come here right now!"

I was working in the hospital that Saturday and did not understand the urgency. I told him, "You have to give me something more to go on to leave work."

My younger son said, "Your son is not breathing."

I said, "What? Have you checked his pulse? Do you need to give him CPR?"

Being a physical therapist kicked in my medical instincts. He said, "Mom, your son is gone."

Dave had committed suicide. At that moment, my heart dropped to the pit of my stomach in shock and disbelief of what I had just heard. I did not want to believe this was true. I felt this numbness that came over my body and I started shivering as those words were absorbed. I became frozen for a moment in a state that was denying this reality. I tried so hard to be in a state of denial, but my heart would not let me stay there. My heart felt the crushing flow of pain rushing through me and I broke down in tears. My coworkers gathered around me as I had to sit down to absorb the words that my son was gone. I could barely get out the words to tell the group that my son was dead. They hugged and embraced me as my body was shaking and my tears were flowing. I was unable to speak clearly. They rallied immediately to help drive me to my youngest son's home.

I arrived at Billy's apartment to find my daughter, son-in-law, grandson, and Billy on the porch. They greeted me with heavy hearts of sorrow and tears as they each hugged me. The police were inside the apartment investigating. There was a policeman who brought me into the living room to sit as they were winding up the investigation. I knew my older son, Dave, was in the next room and I was horrified to think that there was no life in his body. I was still trembling in shock from the loss. The officers were very compassionate to our family. They were getting ready to take his body away. Four of us expressed that we wanted to see him before he left. They asked if we were sure, and we all confirmed that we were. As they wheeled him out of the room on a gurney, they stopped to let us see him one last time. For me, I had to see his body to make it real. The reality was hard to see. I saw he was not there in his body anymore. It was hard to see the indent on his forehead from the pressure of lying face down. I knew my son was not the body I was looking at. This empty body was missing the spirit of my son, his emotions, his humor, his quirky moments, his laughter, and his personality that everyone loved about him. This being who I called my son was not his body that I identified with. There was the spiritual presence I was missing.

I left my other family members to go home. They were coming over shortly after, as they did not want me to be home alone that night. Before they came, I was in the living room shouting out to Dave in anger about him leaving as he did. I shouted at the top of my lungs, grieving over his loss. WHY!? I was so angry at the loss of my son who for ten years had tried to help his stepchildren and the dysfunctional family he had been in.

I thought of suicide and wondered why? I knew my son Dave's story very well and his reason became very apparent. After the first of the year in 2021, he was accused of molestation of a minor. When I heard the news on a cold, icy, and snowy day, I was in disbelief and so was the rest of the family and friends that had known Dave since he was a child or a baby. There was no way that he could have done this. He was raising two girls of his own. One daughter was twenty-one years old, and the other daughter was seventeen. Dave had become a grandfather three months earlier. What we witnessed as a family was him being a great, caring dad to his girls. This accusation to us was surreal and unbelievable to anyone who knew Dave.

Many businesses were closed due to inclement weather and dangerous driving conditions. He was arrested in February and did not know how to contact us, as his cell phone was taken away and he had not memorized our phone numbers. Once he contacted the number where he worked, we found out about his arrest. His bail was originally set at $500,000 with no criminal record in his past. As a family, we realized we had to find him an attorney. My grandson's girlfriend, who worked at a law office, asked around and found a great attorney. He had handled these kinds of cases before, and we retained him to represent my son. The first thing he recognized was that the bail was set too high. He went to court to have Dave's bail lowered, and the judge agreed that it was too high. The judge lowered it to $100,000. The family came up with the money to get him out of jail.

After two weeks of confinement in jail, he was so elated to be out. His sister and oldest daughter were outside when he came to meet them. They took pictures of all the hugs and celebration of him being out of jail, and we knew he did not deserve to spend another moment there.

Dave was so grateful to be free. Being out of jail and able to see family meant the world to him. There were many restrictions made in his bail, including the fact that he could not be around anyone under the age of eighteen. That meant that he could not see his youngest daughter, who was seventeen, or his newborn grandson. He wore an ankle monitor at all times. He could not be on a computer or cell phone that was connected to the internet. He lost the dream job he had worked so hard to achieve.

As months went by, Dave was hopeful in the beginning, but then as trial after trial was postponed and delayed, the process started to weigh him down. The weather conditions and Covid had delayed the judicial process. He began to lose trust and hope in the judicial system. Dave had been doing everything he could to occupy his time. He went to Bible study and to church. He worked out twice a day at the gym. He was so limited by what he could do without breaking his parole. He was unable to attend our family gatherings when children were around. That included big holidays for us, like Easter and the Fourth of July. Dave always seemed to understand and make the best of it. Dave had been staying at his younger brother's apartment for months after the arrest, and Billy had him on suicide watch, but Dave seemed to be willing to fight this case against him. He kept waiting for his arraignment, that never came, in which he was going to plead innocent to this crime. Any evidence that Dave's attorney attempted to enter to prove his innocence was not allowed by the District Attorney. Dave began to lose faith that he would get a fair trial and the only proof they had to convict him was the testimony of a young girl who had many psychological issues.

Dave journaled about his life leading up to his arrest, as I encouraged him to do. He wanted to document everything he had been experiencing, especially the last couple of years. The journal he left behind of his experiences was sad and disheartening. He became a victim of unusual family dynamics in his marriage and with the stepchildren he had helped raise for almost ten years.

Football season always brought Dave to life. It was October 2021, eight months after his arrest, and football season was in full swing. He was a huge Dallas Cowboys fan while his younger brother, Billy, was a big New York Giants fan. Whenever these two teams came together for a game, it was a big event for our family. The weekend was coming up for the two teams to play each other. Most of the family was out of town, and there were no worries about children being around. We decided to have our own weekend of fun with a football party with Dave, Billy, my daughter-in-law Diana, and me. Dave had called and asked if he could come over Friday night instead of Saturday. I said sure. Dave was trying to get the other two to come Friday, also, but they decided to come on Saturday.

That Thursday night before the weekend, Dave, Billy, and Diana were watching Thursday night football. Diana went to bed, and Billy and Dave continued enjoying the game. Billy thought Dave was coming to my house the next day, on Friday, as he was letting everyone think. Billy had him on suicide watch for so many months, and yet Dave had the upper hand. Billy and Diana spent Friday night thinking that Dave had come to stay with me. That is why I got the call on Saturday morning at work. Billy asked if Dave had come to stay the night as he planned. I said, "No, he never showed up."

That was when Billy knew. He sent Diana out of the apartment to see if Dave's car was there. While she was gone, Billy got a special key to open Dave's door, which was locked. Once he opened the door, that was when he saw his brother's body lying face down on the bed. When Diana returned, Billy told her to call the police.

After the police were finished with their investigation, I was given the journal that Dave left. I had encouraged him to write down everything that he remembered during his marriage. He left a "holographic will" that stated his wishes, and at the end, I read his last words, **"I love you all. I did not do what I am accused of. I do not have faith in our legal system. I am not going to prison for a crime I did not commit. I am so sorry. Please forgive me."**

I look at that Saturday when I learned that my son had taken his life and read his last words. I felt so much grief that I had to step back from it. For the first few days, I had to allow myself the space to go through all the shock I was experiencing and the roller coaster of emotions I was feeling. After several days, I was aware my mind was triggering the process of whether I should be angry and bitter toward the young girl who had contributed to this loss. I knew I could not carry the heaviness of blame, anger, and bitterness in my heart. Instead, I looked to Spirit for guidance.

This is an important lesson in healing the deep loss of a child. You cannot heal from a tragedy of this depth without your spirit guiding you if you ever want peace. I reached out to Spirit to help me take this to a level that I could understand.

Spiritually, I was given two choices. I could live with resentment, anger, and bitterness in my heart for a seventeen-year-old who falsely accused him only to get him out of the house, or I could rise above what appeared to be the conditions of fear and the ego to honor Dave's spirit of who he really was in this life. I chose to honor my son's life. In doing that, I had to let go of anyone's perceived guilt toward his death. I had to forgive the journey that led him to take his own life. This was a lot to ask but honoring him was a much higher vibration and a place that I could rest in peace. The other alternative was too heavy for my heart to carry if I wanted to serve the higher good.

Do I miss him? Always. I continue to honor his spirit and all the achievements in his life. One of the highest compliments that was given at his celebration of life service was by a family member who I had asked to speak. He said, "There are only two people I have known in my life that I have never heard them speak a bad word about anyone. One was my Aunt Judy and the other is Dave."

Dave's celebration of life was a beautiful service. He will be remembered as a loving son, father, brother, and friend. I was so grateful for receiving all the love that surrounded us that day. I know he is very alive in spirit and sometimes I can feel him near me, sending me love and embracing me. That is a gift from spirit that I appreciate.

Healing emotional wounds is necessary, and most of the time unpleasant in the beginning and liberating at the end. Remember that what you are seeking lives beyond the unhealed wound. I was grateful that Spirit was preparing me in increments through people who have left me for their transition of life. Experiencing my son's death is the only reason I reached higher. Spirit had been preparing me for what was coming that I could not see. At the level of my spiritual journey now, I can only hold my son in the spirit of love and light of his being. I can be tempted to go back to other feelings, but his life in this space is too meaningful, so I keep this focus, and in that I rest in peace with him and still feel very connected to his spirit.

The discomfort of the feelings that do not support my true being is only temporary. In the healing, the truth reveals itself. My enlightened being shines through and love awakens in the surrender of the negative emotions as I let go. The energy of light flows through me and embraces me as I am lifted higher out of the density of those negative energies. I have a deep sense of gratitude for experiencing the grace of peace. As my consciousness holds the space for the love, compassion, and true joy of the spirit that my son is, I feel honored to be his mother. I know in my heart that while on Earth, he was a true, caring soul and loved to make people laugh and have fun through his being a Misfit; a mascot at the basketball games with the crowds of families at the basketball stadium having fun with the costume he wore and the entertainment he provided. The karaoke nights we had with him leading us on with singing and engaging everyone to get up to sing a song brought so much fun to family and friends. We have carried on with the karaoke that he loved so much and continue to experience the fun that he began when he drew us into it. He left that gift to us. My heart lives with the fun and happy memories of him.

I know that my son, after raising two daughters of his own, always loved life and always held to the positives in life. One of his well-known phrases that he always said when something was negative was, "That's head trash!"

None of us are perfect, but what I do know about my son is that he always sought to love and to be loved.

Dave will live in my heart forever. He was my first son. I could live in the depth of sorrow for what I lost, but I chose to live in the beauty of his spirit. Did he have flaws? Absolutely! Did he have a good heart and spirit? Yes, indeed! Whenever I focus daily on Dave's spirit, I remember what Carla taught me years ago about our kids: "Your children belong to God first and then to you."

"Grief may never end but it changes. It's a passage, not a place to stay. Grief is not a sign of weakness nor a lack of faith. It is the practice of loving deeply." (Author Unknown)

Healing Love Practice

The Awareness:

*Focus on what you want to support as their
memory instead of what you lost.*

When you lose any loved one, how do you honor them?

What do you define their life to mean
that you carry in your heart?

The Affirmation

Divine Love flows through me to elevate my departed loved ones.

CHAPTER 15

The Ultimate Act of Forgiveness

Forgiveness is the act of releasing and freeing the negative energy that binds the spiritual heart. Whether it is self-forgiveness or forgiving others, it carries an emotional power that transcends fear if it comes sincerely through the heart. Beliefs are at the core of what we can forgive and what may feel like unthinkable forgiveness. Forgiveness asks us to reach into our hearts to seek true forgiveness. That is when you lay down your sword of defense from your fear and recognize a source of goodness flowing through you that cannot carry the weight of another wound. You look objectively and honestly at what caused the fear to arise and then look deeply and honestly at the event that disrputed Love.

What we create through our belief system is reflected to us from the outside world. If you think you were betrayed, then there is something you have betrayed within your spirit or a belief that you carry of how people have to present themselves to be acceptable and worthy of love. If you feel someone is attacking you emotionally, then look to see what emotions within yourself are out of balance with your true spirit.

I was ridiculed by friends and family for my spiritual beliefs and practices back in the 1980s. I could easily forgive them teasing me and making me feel unimportant and ridiculous because I knew this was the outside world that was reacting from their lack of awareness of the spiritual world. Their ridicule did not deter me from what I knew in my heart. I could easily let it go. On the other hand, there have been times I had to reach a depth within myself to neutralize my pain. I needed time to reflect and understand the dynamics that were taking place. I can always trace it back to my beliefs if I am completely honest with myself.

As I have grown spiritually, I learned that being truthful with my emotions gave me insights into the awareness about myself and others who were led astray by fear. When you think you have hidden your lies in a deep, dark place never to be discovered, that is when they will surface without you having any control. I thought that my son's death was laid to rest until new discoveries came up that I was not aware of. Confessions of the heart could not lay buried deep for long.

Two years had passed since my son's arrest in February 2021. Lies and misguided truths eventually found their way to the surface and were revealed. The family was deceived by who the whistleblower was that accused Dave of sexual misconduct with a minor. I was in shock to find out it was my granddaughter. Having experienced it herself from one of her mother's boyfriends, she hesitated to call Child Protective Services (CPS), but pressure from her mother and the accuser's boyfriend resulted in the call she made. The learning experience comes later after all the dominos have fallen. This is a monumental lesson to learn that we are so quick to place judgment, we fail to discern whether the situation is the truth or misguided by fear. When you are about to accuse another person of a crime that carries the severity of punishment that this accusation did, you want to make sure that you have solid evidence to back it up. There was no evidence, only lies and deceit were built into a false accusation causing another person's life to be destroyed.

Knowing now that my son was innocent, and yet falsely accused of a crime he did not commit, made forgiveness more challenging.

Dave ended his life knowing that even if he was found innocent, the stigma of the accusations would follow him for the rest of his life. This became a colossal lesson on how false judgment can severely injure another person's life. I am now aware that this kind of accusation is being used more frequently for other reasons than the actual crime. In Dave's case, it was his stepdaughter simply wanting him out the house.

To find the forgiveness, embraced by love, I had to go to the beginning of my granddaughter's life and remember when she was three years old. There was her innocence and pure spiritual heart alive and functioning. Time progressed forward and I could see how the conditioning from her mother changed her perceptions and created limiting beliefs that were fear-based. As she grew older, the fear grew larger and limitations began to set in. Insecurities and doubts became greater. The decisions she made for her life were not based on a foundation of love. The critical decisions for her life's direction were made from fear. Anything good happening in her life did not last long. Circumstances she found herself in and the decisions she made were self-sabotaging and self-destructive. Even though I was aware of the fear conditioning of her life, I understood I had no control over her decisions. Fear had set in its structure so deep that I realized the only thing I could do was love her, hold the vision of her true spirit in my heart, and forgive the ignorance of her actions. Sometimes, we would love to save people from their self-destructive patterns, but then I remembered the only thing I can control and save is myself.

A year after my son's death, I discovered I had breast cancer, a rare form called Paget's Disease. I went in knowing something was wrong. After a mammogram and ultrasound, the suspected diagnosis came and was confirmed with a biopsy. Luckily, I caught it at stage zero, but it required surgery. My daughter took me to the hospital on the day of surgery, and stayed until I was ready to go home. I felt my two children and daughter-in-law supporting me. The "c" word was something others were uncomfortable talking about. I was okay with that. My focus was on healing from the surgery and moving forward until a week later, when I received a call from my surgeon that she had to go back for another surgery because the pathologist reported that some of my margins were not clean. My heart dropped for a moment, and then I realized that I had to accept and flow with what was needed. This time, the surgeon had a pathologist in the operating room so that she would be certain that she had clean margins. It was done. The pathologist confirmed it.

The challenge I had to face after the second surgery was my grandson's rehearsal dinner the next night and his wedding the following day. I could not conceive the possibility of missing any of it. I attended the rehearsal dinner and the wedding. As word spread, the ones who knew of my recent surgeries were amazed that I was there for the wedding. Afterward, I experienced weeks of radiation, and then it was over. I reflected on this experience and the life that was directing me to move forward. To do this, I had to reach deep into my heart to forgive my son for the decision he made to take his own life. My cancer was about the lack of nurturing of my inner spirit to complete the healing and forgiveness of the circumstances that brought a sadness of my son leaving the way he did. Love leaves no stone unturned. I learned that with difficult situations we face in life, sometimes there are many layers of forgiveness.

Ultimate forgiveness is moving through the layers of emotions that have impacted your life from an experience. The more profound the experience, the more layers that will come up over time. Sometimes, these incidents come when least expected to throw you totally off guard and make you wonder afterwards what had happened to create this? I found myself in a situation eight months ago with my sister's family where a disconnection happened after a circumstance of nature created an experience where no family member was involved, only beloved animals. I was not happy in the environment I was in, and yet I did not act soon enough to avoid the acts of nature that followed. I was not aware of the urgency to move out and find my own place. I was making plans after the first of the year to find my own home, and these plans were discussed between my sister and me. I was aware of my uncomfortable situation building. I needed to move on but did not understand it should be sooner than later, as my sister had asked for a six-month notice. Sometimes, life intervenes on your behalf to move things forward more quickly.

I had been living with my sister in her home for three years, wanting to be there so she would not be alone. I was the younger one and knew my sister was carrying a heavy responsibility of taking over her company after her husband's death. Being an empath, I naturally wanted to help her. The storm coming began to build during the last year I was there. The forces of nature came into play and created a situation that separated the family.

In January, on a cold winter evening around dusk, my dog, Starsky, walked toward me on the back patio. There was a look on his face that made me come toward him. As I was observing him, I attempted to figure out what was wrong. I discovered he had blood all over his body and one eye was squinting. I could see the marks around his eye. Starsky looked defeated and sad. My sister was coming home through the back yard, and I told her that something had happened to Starsky. I took him inside and got towels that I wetted to wash the blood off of his body. I looked at his eye and realized that it was a bite. It appeared that he had encountered a predator. I tried to determine what had happened. I knew that I needed to go out with a flashlight to see if I could find evidence of what had attacked him. My sister called her son-in-law who lived next door. He came over with his flashlight and I pointed to where I saw something laying on the ground. He went over and discovered it was his cat that was dead. An immediate conclusion was drawn as he came toward me to tell me that Starsky had killed their cat. I was shocked, as I knew that Starsky felt a loss for the cat because he had always played security guard for her whenever she was out. He always felt a need to protect her. In the past several years, he alerted the family with his barking when the cat was outside and they did not know. I knew he loved the cat. She was not so fond of him, though, because he always called her out.

This set in motion the feelings from my sister's family that had to face the death of their cat. Starsky was accused of killing the cat and my dog was no longer welcome there. My sister was placed in an awkward situation with her daughter and family. I did not want any discord between them. There were coyotes that roamed in the neighborhood, and Starsky may have been protecting the cat from a predator. I will never know, as no one witnessed what really happened. I do know that Starsky was not aggressive and was safe around children and babies. Starsky was attacked by something. Whether it was a coyote or the cat attacking him causing him to defend himself, we will never know. After the incident, I took him to a familiar place that he loved to board, Lucky Dog Ranch. This was the place where I originally adopted him when he was a puppy. The couple who owned the ranch were informed of the situation and they gladly received Starsky into their care while I had to urgently determine where I would go.

I found a rental home since it was faster than going through the process of buying. I was shocked and devastated initially by the fact that Starsky and I had to leave abruptly, but I knew in my heart there was a reason I was called so quickly out of the environment I was living in. Within two weeks I had chosen a home, and the location was perfect for me. On the day I had movers scheduled, there was an ice and snowstorm that delayed the move. I kept in touch with Starsky and how he was doing at Lucky Dog Ranch. I was told that Starsky was having a hard time walking. I realized that whatever he experienced that night had taken its toll on his spirit. As the ice was melting and before the movers came, I went to see Starsky. Jeff, the owner, had to carry him outside because he could barely walk anymore. I spent an hour outside with Jeff and Starsky in his yard, and I was sad and heartbroken knowing that it would be the last time I would see and spend time with him. Starsky lay beside me, and I rubbed and petted him, which always gave him comfort. Watching him struggle to attempt to stand was heartbreaking to witness. I had to leave, knowing that the next day my son-in-law was taking Starsky to his vet to lay him to rest on the same day I was moving into my new home. All of these things happening simultaneously was extremely emotional for me, but I had to reach deep into my faith to move forward, because the disconnection of my sister's family was a reality that I had to reflect on. I came to understand that the family animals involved were the blade cutters of the separation that came. I recognized that this was a divine intervention experience. I grieved the loss of my dog, just as my sister's family lost their cat. I knew that spirit had set this in motion for a reason. My family has been separated since that time. I accepted there was a deeper underlying reason and allowed months to pass for it to be revealed.

I have found peace living in my own home and being away from family who had different areas of focus than what I was moving toward. When the storm arose and moved through, the after-effect for me was settling into a place that better supported my life. I let go of needing to care for others and focused on my own life to give myself the support and love that I needed.

The interesting result of forgiveness was that when family or people close to you leave your life, new friends come in to fill the void. I have closure now with the incident that separated me from my sister's family. I learned when you are no longer in the energetic alignment that creates connection, the relationships no longer make sense. It is similar to two energy fields that become misaligned. Your mirrors to each other's lives no longer reflect. There can still be love between family members as the process of rebuilding the relationships heals.

I received clarity on the reason I was pulled out of that environment so quickly. I was writing this book and the energy of living there was not supporting the energy I needed to complete the book. After moving and settling into my home, I was able to leave the distractions of their lives and give the energy and focus I needed to complete my book.

The discovery of my granddaughter calling CPS on my son, my breast cancer, and the disconnection of my sister's family all happened last year. These were all deeply emotional situations that I moved through because of my alignment and connection with Spirit. I had to put into action everything I have taught in this book to move through each situation. I am grateful for my connection with Spirit that helps me move through challenging situations.

You know when you have found your alignment and peace. Forgiveness is the key to your freedom. The energy that binds you is released and is free for more creative, uplifting experiences. The walk of trust with the divine nature of who we are to direct and guide our journey of Love is rewarded with fulfillment of love and peace within.

Human life is a journey that is challenging and rewarding at the same time. The key is to always see the value in what you give. There is a human element that needs forgiveness, and you will find it within yourself. Life outside of yourself is only your mirror within.

What are you having a hard time forgiving? The life we seek is Love, and only through forgiveness can we truly live. Life on Earth is so short from the perspective of the spiritual world. We see it as a long journey. What is real? It is whatever time it takes to find the true enlightenment of our hearts through forgiveness.

Healing Love Practice

The Awareness

Forgiveness is the ultimate healer of our emotional wounds.

What have you experienced in your life
that needed forgiveness to heal?

How has your forgiving nature allowed
re-connection with others?

My Affirmation

I am moved by the indwelling love within
to see beyond fear and forgive.

CHAPTER 16

Putting Our House in Order

As we clear our inner world from the clutter of fears, doubts, and judgments, we begin to arrange our inner home with the sentiments of a loving and caring spiritual heart as the foundation. We then begin to furnish our newly-awakened awareness with uplifting beliefs that will serve as the framework of the interior of our inner home. The colors we select are the ones that bring a sense of warmth and comfort that evoke a feeling of peacefulness. The scents of nature remind us of the beauty they represent as we dwell within the walls of this sacred place in divine connection. I envision a special room where I go to comfortably sit while I resolve any conflicting experiences of the day that might have gone against the harmonious flow of Love that I support. There is a sense of support and guidance that occupies this space. This inner world I have created is the place from which I receive all I need to direct me on the course of life that will serve my highest good and give outwardly to others who cross my path.

To achieve this place, we must overcome our fears. That is the only thing that separates us from our true nature as loving, unified beings. Our internal emotional wounds that we carry keeps us separate. To overcome fear, we must understand the nature of it. Fear's nature is to limit and pull us back from moving forward or not appreciating the differences that make each of us unique and special. Its nature restricts what we desire, wish, or dream. Fear can diminish our true spirit and make us feel less than who we really are. We can lose value in what we think we can accomplish. As we heal those fear-based wounds, we will come to feel more connected to each other and the world we live in. I would not have reached the depth of understanding of my spirit had I not had the journeys that guided me to understand my true spiritual nature.

Your journey will not be the same as mine. It is not supposed to be. Your life is uniquely your own, just like mine. What we all share in common is our spirit and Love. This is universal. If we can appreciate our differences as well as what we have in common, we have the chance to create a peaceful, loving place to experience life.

When we can associate and become aware in our lives of what is love-driven versus what is fear-driven, then we can make better choices for our lives. For me, the true journey of life is to discover the full potential of the gifts and talents we have and share them to uplift the world. Once these gifts and talents come to life, spiritual guidance will assist us in using these talents for the greater good of humanity.

I admire the strength and courage of each soul here, no matter what they may be facing. Through our struggles and letdowns, it is important to remember that it is only temporary. That knowing has sustained me through any challenges in my life. The fear and unhealed wounds are short-lived if we allow them to surface and discover new spiritual truths that will offset them. We continually rise every day to move forward toward what we seek and what we want in our lives. Our beliefs that we are not enough begin to fade as we gain confidence in our vision of what we are moving toward. We are now acutely aware that what we dwell on most will draw us closer. The importance of our choice between love and fear will be clear as situations come into our lives.

We want to experience joy in our life. Don't save your joy for retirement or any other reason than to be in it now. Lee Harris, whom I have followed because his heart is immensely genuine, loving, and caring, and the Zs, whom he channels, gave some information I heard and took note of. The Zs said, "Joy is five times more powerful than fear. And yet, fear is five times more powerfully sown into the collective than joy."

That statement was mind-boggling! I knew this statement to be true when it was spoken because I have seen how fear desperately works to divert our focus on problems we need to solve, what is lacking in our lives, and guides us to dwell in heaviness so that we drown our joy. We have been conditioned in fear and are in the process of deconditioning our minds and hearts from fear to love. We must begin to tune in to the joy that is our birthright from God.

My spiritual journey has instilled the importance and value of self-love. Lack of self-love made me feel separate from others for a long time. I went too long in life not realizing how valuable it was. I had to release the harshness and judgment I had placed on myself. For me, it was always easier to see the beauty in other people, and yet, I was always too critical of myself. The beauty that is unfolding for me is that I am making a conscious effort every day to recognize and acknowledge the beauty and love of my own being. As I continue to live with self-love, I have moments that come to challenge it every once in a while.

When we take each piece of what makes us whole, it all comes down to mastering fear, growth in self-love, understanding and appreciating our differences, and allowing joy into our experiences to bring us those uplifting moments. Our lives are far greater than we can possibly imagine. If you ever experience wanting to move forward and you feel hesitation because of the unknown, believe that you can move forward through this fear that tries to hold you back. Tony Robbins taught me and all who have attended his programs to "defy the odds!" What this meant for me was to move through my fears that were trying to hold me back. Ever since I learned this, I have used it throughout my life to achieve all that I have accomplished.

I have carried a dream in my heart since the early 1990s of becoming an author. I let it go for years, giving myself all the reasons I could not achieve it, and writing a book to help others was too far out of my reach. I questioned myself and wondered if this was imaginary or real.

In January of 2020, I was in Cancun, Mexico, celebrating a family member's milestone birthday. There was a large group attending the week-long celebration. One evening, my sister and I were sitting on the balcony of my hotel room having our last nightcap before bed. We were enjoying the clear night air with the multitude of stars above us. I was star gazing when my sister asked me what was wrong. She told me that I did not seem happy. I had to take a moment to be completely honest with myself and realized she was right. There was something missing within me that I could not put my finger on at the time.

After our return, I began to go within to find what seemed to be an emptiness; something unfulfilled that brought the sadness. With the beginning of a new decade, I knew there was something on the horizon that I wanted to fulfill. I opened myself to receive whatever that might be. I became more involved with self-growth programs online, because two months after our trip Covid hit the country and life as we knew it changed. That same year, I rediscovered Alan Cohen when I was given a spiritual nudge to check out his website to see what he was doing. I attended one of his online courses and then discovered that he had a program for holistic life coaches. This intrigued me, so I signed up for the next class.

I went through the training, and as I was learning the coaching skills some old baggage began to surface. My fears were definitely challenging; imposter syndrome was the biggest challenge for me. I was not the only one in our group who was feeling it. As we each moved through the awkwardness of our new coaching skills, we began to have new insights and breakthroughs. The success of moving through the discomforts that fear presented gave us confidence. The program was a cleansing for us to be open to receive as we tuned into our spirit for guidance through our coaching sessions. During this time, I also began doing channeled writing. This reconnection was helpful, and I received insight and comforting messages from the writings.

After we graduated and passed our final exam, I decided to take a trip to visit one of the coaches I met who lives in San Diego. Reconnecting months later, was a refreshing and happy time for us. I spent a long weekend there in the fall of 2021, and on the last day we decided to have readings from a local medium who Kathy and I knew. Luckily, she had openings for both of us.

When I had my reading, I asked to speak with my "spiritual council," as I sensed there was a group of them. During the reading with this council, I was told that I would be writing a book. They even gave me the name of the book: *Love Heals All Wounds*. I was taken aback by this new information, but I appreciated all the inspiration shared during the reading.

The next morning was the day I was leaving, and I awoke earlier than I had intended. I went into the living room and sat in a cozy chair where Kathy did her meditations. I began my meditation and then was guided to write in my journal what was being given to begin my journey of writing my book. This is what I wrote:

The Awakening Heart

In ancient times, souls of people reached up into the skies asking for that which was void in their essence, their state of being. In their human form, they had lost sight of the light of their true being. These humans were searching for the energy of their own sensitivity, the true nature of Love and all that it embraced. It was in these times that Love revealed itself and filled Light into their human form to experience and share with the world.

If you believe that Earth is your only existence, then you will live the Earth ways. The illusion of time, circumstances, and experiences are for human growth and will be experienced whether you are solid in the Earth ways or seeking beyond Earth. There are many who have learned there is more than what appears before them in what their human form portrays. This is when the spiritual journey of enlightenment begins. You become a seeker of Truth.

The incubation period of my book began in the fall of 2021, and by February 2022, fears and doubts arose. At this point, I am questioning whether this is real for me to continue writing this book. Doubts are growing. I am overcoming insecurities within myself to feel that I am worthy to write this book. I want this so much, and I do understand that any insecurities must arise and be released for me to keep going. One evening, when I was reaching to Spirit to guide and help me, this is the message I received:

We are chosen to awaken the souls who live on Earth who are attempting to find their way. We would say that as you reach out to souls who are searching for answers through your words, these ones will find their way into a more productive and supported life. If you could see for one human soul that their life transforms for what you participated and helped with, seeing their beauty before they could see it and moving toward greater love for self, then all is worth the effort. We stand before you to open your heart to new ideas that will assist on your journey. These beings who are assisted with raising their vibration will come to see their world in a new light. You are here to create a new world of enlightenment that is moving faster as time goes on. The message you are given is the wave of consciousness that has vibrational qualities lifting you upward. This book is guided by a higher consciousness with the words that are printed that will bring peace and enlightenment.

This was given for me to keep going, and I did.

Anything new brings insecurities and fears about what you have not experienced or demonstrated. This is a given. This is how we grow within ourselves. I hope that somehow your journey is enlightened by what you have read, and that you experience your own unique journeys that build your awareness of the spirit that lives within you. I share with you this inspiration I wrote one night when I was feeling everything coming together as I reflected on my life and the gifts given to me by Spirit:

> *What do I love about Spirit and my journey with you? You have supported me in ways that I could not have possibly imagined. You have given me a journey of a lifetime. Many ups and downs, but the growth that came from that has been amazing. I am truly grateful for all that I have experienced, but I do know now that you have always been with me, even in the times I could not see or feel you. I do not even know how to repay you, but what comes to mind is to live the best life I can at any given moment. That is what you have taught me. Always be the best version of me that I can be at any time in my life. I have worked so hard in this life to experience and grow beyond my boundaries and limitations, to find the true nature of my being, to help those that suffer to find peace, and to give to those I love as well as those in need. I truly feel at peace with who I AM and what I have given. And with this, I rest in peace.*

Many times, we are not aware of what our masterpiece in life will be until we move beyond the fears that bind us. Love will set us free from the boundaries that are within the walls of our hearts to open and express what we are here to give. As we practice being aware of what draws us away from the Love that we seek, our fears will have less power over our lives. This is the time that you will be the director of your life, keeping it on a steady course to navigate what you want to create and give to help others. We are here to help each other achieve whatever we can envision to bring love, support, and awareness, making our lives more enriched with Love's presence.

Healing Love Practice

The Awareness:

***When we recognize our power to be in our rightful place,
it will be achieved.***

What have you wanted and sought to achieve
that brought challenges and fears?

What were the empowering thoughts that
moved you beyond fear to achieve this?

My Affirmation

I claim this as the perfect place and
perfect time to achieve what I want.

CHAPTER 17

You are the Creator and the Salvation of Your Life

We create our life experiences through our belief system, hopefully based on what we want instead of what we don't want, no matter which religion we may follow. Our belief system resides in the core of our being, and what you experience every day is a result of that belief system and your focus, which is either love- or fear-based. I have a friend who is a beautiful, loving soul who is having marital problems again. She continually draws men into her life that she falls in love with, and then that love does not support love from them. She has always been let down by the men that she has married. Does this problem belong to her or the men she married? It belongs to her. She has not fully embraced love within herself and seeks to find love outwardly. She is a victim of fear and is blinded by it.

As we were talking about her recent marriage that is dissolving, I asked her why she desperately wants to make it work, even when her heart knows that it is a lost cause. She responded that even when she was being deceived, those were some of their happiest times. She also shared that without her husband and her children, most of whom are grown, she does not have any interest that she can think of that brings her any kind of joy or excitement. That is when I realized that she had just found the root of her problem. We can't depend on the outside world for our happiness and fulfillment. We will always come up empty.

To heal wounds from the past, we must first understand about the spiritual heart, created by God, that was given to us at birth when we left the spiritual world to take on a human body. There is not a manual about our spiritual heart being the creator and the salvation that flows with us into this new physical form. We are born into the world, and at that time, the only things we have to guide us are our parents, siblings, or friends who also did not receive a manual. I want to propose how this manual, if it did exist, might read to help in understanding the nature of the spiritual heart and to assist in navigating the life you are moving toward as you heal your inner wounds. It all begins with you, a spiritual being, trying to figure out a human world, but now with a beacon of light to help navigate the heart and soul.

1. **The spiritual heart knows only Love and flows with that energy. Remember that Love cannot be opposed by any negative energy, otherwise it creates a wound.**

    We are the creators of our emotional wounds whenever we veer from the harmonious flow of Love. There is always a human factor, a situation, experience, or something outside of us that we respond to that we think is real. It becomes our fear that we keep inside until we learn and grow beyond it.

2. **You are the creator of your interactions with anyone, and how these play out will depend on your beliefs that flow with each one. Your beliefs are the foundation of how you perceive your world.**

    If you experience something that you do not like, go within to find what you believe brought you the experience. Many times, your beliefs are about how you feel about yourself. The outside world is just reflecting that back to you. You have the power to transform your beliefs as you experience spiritual enlightenment and awareness.

3. **When you react to anyone in anger, reflect on the underlying cause. (What hurt you?)**

Anger is fear under pressure. We react in an unexpected moment when we feel threatened or attacked emotionally. This happens to all of us at one time or another. You can feel your energy shift the moment it happens. Your energy drops and it doesn't feel good. You may choose to wrestle with it or justify it, but your soul will wait patiently for you to become weary of the battle. Always ask questions. What is this experience trying to tell me? What am I supposed to learn from this? What is my belief that set this in motion?

4. **Discover your triggers that make you have negative responses to improve your outcome and minimize your wound count.**

Encounters with family or friends may trigger unexpected emotions that cause a reaction that does not come from Love. Sometimes they do it innocently, and some may be intentional. This is the time to recognize those triggers, so that when they come, you can have a choice with how you react. Those are your unhealed wounds that you need to address. Awareness and forgiveness are the keys to unraveling the web that started the anger, sometimes many years ago.

5. **Any negative belief can be transformed into a positive belief by right of your own consciousness.**

You are the creator and, also, the salvation of your life. *You are the one who gives life to whatever you create or experience. The divine* *order in your life is played out for you to become aware of what you want or don't want, what serves you or not, and what is in your highest good if you seek it. Your life is one of a kind. It is yours to play out however you wish. Remember that the people in your life who challenge you the most are the ones that love you and believe in you the most to help you grow beyond fear.*

When we take time to focus on what uplifts our spirit, we are given loving vibrations that can help us remember the positive qualities that abide within, which are love, support, guidance, and inspiration. We have so much unused potential within us that is available if we dare to pursue it. Many times, we are conditioned by fear through society and the distraction of the outside world, and we lose sight of the treasures that are awaiting within.

As I practiced these spiritual truths, I had an experience one evening as I was in bed drifting off to sleep. I was in that space of being relaxed but not fully asleep, when I felt myself leaving my body and rising above it. I did not understand what I was experiencing. I panicked in fear, and I started spinning around in circles so fast and could not make it stop. I was afraid because I had no control. As I finally let go of the fear, it stopped. Shortly after that, I saw my spiritual teacher, Carla, and told her about the experience. She told me that if it happened again, to relax and experience what it was giving me. To trust it. I took her advice, and the next time it happened I did not react in fear. I lifted out of my physical body and felt my etheric body floating around the room. My consciousness was aware of being out of my physical body. I continued to have multiple conscious out-of-body experiences. This happened during my early seeking of spiritual awareness.

Out-of-body experiences are not uncommon for people who have been involved in serious, life-threatening accidents or people close to death. I was at a dinner one evening with the staff of the Transitional Learning Center when the subject of out-of-body experiences came up. The psychologists were accustomed to having conversations with their head injury clients who described having out-of-body experiences after their accident. One of the psychologists who was sitting across the table from me mentioned that none of his patients could describe what it felt like to come back into their physical body. I was excited to tell him, because it was a distinctive experience I remembered. Coming back into my physical body from my etheric body was like a vacuum suctioning me back, and it was very fast. I believe that these out-of-body experiences were letting me know that I was more than my physical body. I was being given an introduction into my newly-awakening spiritual consciousness. As I continued to learn about being the creator and salvation of my own life, more truths of inspiration came.

6. **You have better chances of enhancing your spiritual heart with daily connection and communication.**

   Connection and love with your spiritual heart is very much needed. Let go of the outside world and have a moment with yourself. Your internal world needs your attention more than the outside world. This will build and grow as you connect daily, because your inner world needs to understand your truest intentions so it can direct your life in helping you to achieve your goals and dreams.

7. **When you don't know how to handle a negative experience that is pulling you down and you need help, ask for divine intervention.**

   Ask and you shall receive. Turn this situation over to spirit and ask how to interpret it to have understanding and awareness. Open yourself to receive the truth. The truth will give you the understanding you need to forgive and release the experience.

8. Check in with yourself to see how you feel every day. What are your highs and lows? Be your own cheerleader for your spiritual heart.

    You are building awareness in your life every day you check in. How did your day go? You are the only one who can answer that question. What did you experience that uplifted you? What was the energy drain of the day? Stay in touch daily with your emotions and grow to understand what makes your day great. That is the way we learn about the true nature of our inner being.

9. Create something special for your spiritual heart that says, "I love you, feel you, and appreciate you."

    Acknowledge your spiritual heart and you may receive an epiphany moment! These are moments when you don't know physically what you just experienced, but your spiritual heart and emotions are aware of it. Take it in and absorb it. This is a gift from the spiritual world. Even on an ordinary day there are smiles, kind words, and connections with others you respond to. Give appreciation and gratitude for the connection with your spiritual heart.

10. As you increase awareness of your inner nature of Love and value, your blessings will multiply.

    This happens spontaneously as you open and connect with your inner presence of Love. You will become a magnet to draw new experiences into your life. Your spiritual heart will be very connected with you. You will be acutely aware of anything outside of yourself that attempts to oppose it. Your mission will be daily connection to keep this Love alive within you.

11. Gratitude brings more loving responses and rewards than dwelling in fear.

Your focus is very important, no matter what life brings your way. Focusing on anything fearful that comes to you draws you away from love and gratitude. Be careful of what you choose to focus on. Fear is an energy drainer. Love and gratitude are energy builders.

I have learned when I think negatively, I easily become depressed if I continue to dwell on that negativity. Society conditions us to be negative thinkers because it focuses on what is wrong. I had to decondition myself out of that life. This does not happen overnight. Deconditioning fear takes daily effort, awareness, and insight with a belief system conditioned with Love. An interesting, but true concept, if you think about is that we were trained to think the worst first. Just like the old phrase, "Expect the worst and hope for the best," we have the ability to reframe this to, "Expect the best and the worst will not exist."

12. When you are depressed, your wounds are running your life.

Sometimes you may feel as if you have been defeated and there is no way out. That is your defeated voice. It has little substance in your life. You are so much more than what you are allowing yourself to experience. This is a time when you think you are giving up, but you are just beginning. You don't know how to deal with what you are experiencing. That is depression. How do you move out? Start with gratitude for everything in your life. What if you have nothing to be grateful for? Start with something small, a kernel of something, and it will build and grow. Gratitude will lead you out of depression.

13. **Fear is an illusion and becomes an emotional wound if left unattended.**

We always have opportunities to address our fears. Sometimes, when a fear appears that is greater than what you can deal with, let go. Ask for spiritual guidance to help you. This is so much better than shoving it down emotionally to become another one of your inner wounds. If you place the fear aside to focus on your inner being and your spiritual heart, you will be given insight as to the truth in the purpose of the fear. When you can do this, your wound count will start to decrease.

14. **Focus on what uplifts your spirit each day.**

A great beginning to each day is to focus on gratitude, and you will feel your energy start to rise. Focus on what makes you happy, whether it is a loved one, a friend, or a special animal. It could also be an environment that makes you come alive. Become more aware of the moments in your day that uplift you. You have permission to build and discover as you go.

15. **Create what brings joy in your life.**

Sometimes, joy may seem hard to come by. As you connect more and more with your inner being, joy will arise from within you. You will find yourself absent of fear and enjoying the things you love. As you become the receiver of love, so does joy follow. The key to healing is to overcome fear and restore it with the Love that is present within you. Joy will be there to greet you.

16. **When in doubt, reach for the higher version of yourself to ask the questions you are struggling with, and the answer will reveal itself.**

Great advice is given to the learner who is in the process of connecting with their inner self. Connecting with the highest version of yourself gives you more insight into what will benefit you the most. As you grow spiritually, there will become a higher version than the previous one. Keep climbing the ladder and soon you will connect with your spiritual heart that will guide you the rest of your life. As you grow spiritually, so does your inner being of awareness.

Take a moment to grab your journal to answer these questions. Go within and be honest with yourself. This belongs to no one else but you. This is your journey to connect with your spirit.

1. What is a fear emotion that you have felt that made you want to retreat from a situation you were in?

2. Not being able to retreat from the situation, what resource did you use, based in Love, that gave you clarity?

3. What is a loving response that you can give to someone who has said something hurtful?

4. What triggers you to feel that you have to defend your choice of something indulgent?

5. What negative belief have you discovered that is not true? What new belief took its place?

6. When you want something, what thoughts do you reflect on that will manifest it?

7. Do you ever step back from a situation that makes you confused and ask for clarification?

8. Do you ever help yourself move out of a stressful or depressing situation?

9. When have you thought someone hurt your feelings only to find out it was how they felt about themselves?

10. What do you enjoy experiencing that makes you feel very alive inside?

11. When have you needed to reach really deep to find an answer that you were unsure of and you received the answer?

12. When do you feel the most joy in your life?

The nature of the beast you are attempting to conquer are your fears and emotional wounds. There is nothing outside of yourself to conquer. This is the illusion of Earth. We think it is out there, but it is really inside each one of us. There is no win or lose. The quality of your life is dependent on the connection, Love, and awareness of your spiritual nature, your spiritual heart, and the self-realization that your whole journey has been about how you have grown internally. There is no punishment for having negative energy or feelings. They are always there to serve you. As you become aware of the nature of the spiritual heart, your consciousness will be lifted higher. As your awareness sharpens with inner growth of your spiritual heart, the negative only serves to help you learn and grow to connect with your true spiritual nature. That is the end game, to flow with the natural spirit that is you.

The following is a short version to reference for gentle reminders as you build and grow your inner consciousness, awareness, and growth toward what you truly seek in a loving, divinely-guided world.

Cheat Sheet for Expanding the Spiritual Heart

- There is only LOVE. Anything other than Love is fear (illusion).

- There is no right or wrong. We all make mistakes. Learn from the lessons if there is healing and forgiveness.

  - The only evil that exists is fear by right of our own consciousness.

- Give love and seek forgiveness when you or others appear to trespass that love.

  - When in pain, which we all endure over the course of our lifetime, be loving and gentle with yourself.

- When you believe in yourself, your spiritual heart will be supporting and uplifting.

  - The more positive focus you give yourself, the more positive energy will be attracted to you.

  - Help others by seeing the best in them and support that vision for them.

  - Create joyful moments that uplift you.

  - Always seek to express the higher version of yourself in any situation.

All levels of our being are affected by our spiritual heart. Mentally, physically, and emotionally, the interactions and experiences of our lives are influenced by our actions and reactions to what we experience. Our true power lies within ourselves to heal the wounds from the past and all the experiences that have hurt us or caused emotional trauma.

This is the beauty of our experiences. We are the creator of our own kingdom on Earth, which is driven by our inner self's choices of what we would create and serve. We will all experience doubt, fear, dis-ease, and love, some more than others. You came here with a plan for your life to fulfill. You are also the salvation of your life when you grow to understand the true nature of love and forgiveness within. You do not ever come to Earth randomly. We all come here with a life purpose. During our experiences, whatever they might be, we discover this purpose if we keep growing internally. Sometimes, life can appear to lead you astray, but there is always purpose in whatever you experience to move on. Live life the way it is meant for you to achieve your highest good.

Healing Love Practice

The Awareness:

The spiritual heart is the foundation from which my life flows.

What has your spiritual heart taught
you with your experiences in life?

What awareness did you discover that brought
you closer to your spiritual heart?

My Affirmation

My spiritual heart abides in me and supports my journey.

CHAPTER 18

Spiritual Concepts for Reference in a Crisis

There were many times during the years of my spiritual journey when there was only one thought I could hold to in faith when I found myself surrounded by fear. This one belief that allowed me to pass through my fear was: "Above all that I am experiencing around me, I stand believing that God's Love is the only thing I truly know to be real." I diligently focused on this belief during times when my fears felt like an overpowering presence.

There have been many spiritual truths that assisted me in fearful times that I have accumulated over many years of spiritual study. I have come to believe that every great teacher had a great teacher. I feel blessed with the knowledge given to me directly or handed down by these teachers. The spiritual philosophy contained within the ideas were given to help us remember what we truly already know.

Carla Gordan introduced me to the books of some of the most spiritual, masterful minds of our times, such as *The Science of Mind* by Ernest Holmes, *The Power of Decision* by Raymond Charles Barker, and *Power Through Constructive Thinking* by Emmett Fox. The books that I was guided to in the 1980s which increased my curiosity and wanting to know more about the spiritual world were books such as *Beyond Death, Visions of the Other Side* and *There Is a River, The Story of Edgar Cayce* by Edgar Cayce and *Born to Heal* by Ruth Montgomery. The messages that each teacher and author carried are universal, reaching out to everyone. I am grateful to these enlightened souls for their contribution and dedication to the belief that we are capable of achieving a higher level of consciousness. This consciousness has helped me move through my inner wounds and unexpected fears that pop up for me to address and move through, now more easily than in the past.

The following spiritual truths and ideas for contemplation of your consciousness have helped me stay neutral in my fear and crisis situations I have endured over the course of my spiritual journey. When I am not reacting in fear, I am able to have a clearer vision of my experience with Love. This is what my spiritual teacher, Carla Gordan, taught me. I have defined what each statement meant for me in my spiritual understanding.

1. **God never takes me half of the way.**

   In my healing process, I remember that God stays with me to the end.

   He does not help me partway through and then forget me.

   Fear can make me feel like there is a momentary loss of connection.

   This statement helps me remember that I am never alone.

2. **I am the deliverer of my crisis, creating the opening for my solution.**

   When I can stay centered with focus on a divine lesson, the answer is there.

Usually, a crisis is created to help me see something that I would not see otherwise.

I create the opening by looking for the good in the situation.

3. **A way of changing who I am is to change the *idea* of who I am.**

Who I think I am and who I am in truth are not always the same.

The idea of who I am is changing as I change.

4. **Anger is fear under pressure.**

When I react in anger, I know I am responding in fear.

I seek to understand what is placing pressure on my fear and the nature of that fear.

The pressure I am feeling is disharmony with my true nature.

5. **The Mind of God is never confused.**

Mind is thought, intellect, emotion, and creativity all flowing in perfect harmony.

There is no fear that exists in the Mind of God.

Confusion is only misunderstanding the truth.

6. **There is no sin, but a mistake; no punishment, but a consequence.**

Sin is a fear-based judgement of an action that has a need to punish.

Out of fear, there is a mistake, and the consequence rights that mistake.

Our growing sensitivity lifts us out of these fears to understanding, forgiveness, and release.

7. **Suffering is not an experience of God.**

   Suffering is a belief in lack and self-punishment that is fear-driven.

   Suffering means I am attempting to cleanse my indiscretions and pain through fear.

   Forgiveness and self-love replace suffering by defusing the fear.

8. **One way out of pain is knowledge.**

   Knowledge provides information that leads to understanding.

   Pain is fear-based and lacking knowledge and truth.

   Pain seeks revenge and justification.

   Understanding leads to forgiveness. Always seek understanding.

9. **We move from opinion to knowledge, knowledge to wisdom, wisdom to understanding illuminated by God.**

   Opinion is knowing part of the situation or person.

   Knowledge is knowing both sides.

   Wisdom is seeing the whole picture and understanding its nature.

10. **When you can say the problem in one sentence, the solution is there.**

    When I can focus honestly on what I am attempting to avoid, I can see the answer.

    Problems are created from not wanting to face the truth or responsibility.

    What I am attempting to control is creating the problem.

11. **This has come to pass.**

    This helps me remember to let go of fear.

When I feel fear, my action is to be centered in divine Love, acknowledge what I am feeling, and refrain from holding or controlling. What I am releasing is an untrue image of myself.

12. What I know myself to be, I AM.

I stand believing in a higher image of myself than what I have been in my past.

As I continue to walk with love in my heart, I will keep discovering the value of the inner treasures that dwell within me.

I am a living example of what I want to be spiritually, emotionally, mentally, and physically.

13. Intuition is Spirit knowing Itself. Opinion is our estimate of reality.

My intuition is the doorway to communication with my spirit and oneness with God and the world.

Here is where I clearly see and hear the truth of my reality.

Opinions are beliefs or judgments that reflect what appears to be on the surface.

Opinions reflect what I want to see in fear. Reflections of truth are what I see from spirit.

14. Freedom to the wise, chains to the fools. (Derivative of a famous Voltaire quote)

Wisdom is the understanding of what I have learned and being responsible for what I create.

Knowledge brings understanding. Understanding brings wisdom. The whole opens to freedom of self.

The chains are the limitations I create when I see with limited vision and hear only what supports my fear.

The chains are broken when I open to the truth and allow the full spectrum of my spirit to speak.

15. We are imprisoned by old, limited thought, and freed by new, enlightened thought.

Thoughts based in fear limit my creative expression.

When I am conscious of my thoughts, I can recognize the ones that take away from my goodness.

I have the ability to change and re-create what I am thinking.

My positive thoughts create freedom in my expression.

16. The Universe is Mind as thought and can be elevated by new thought.

My thoughts manifest as form.

What I choose to believe becomes real in its reflection to me.

What manifests before me now can change as my thoughts change.

17. Facing my greatest fear can give me my greatest achievement.

The greater the fear I face, the greater the hidden treasure that lies beneath the fear.

I face my fear with the confidence that good comes to me in the end.

Facing my fear is my deliverance into Love's presence.

18. I control my destiny. This belief can change the world.

My destiny becomes fulfilled through the choices I make.

I am divinely guided to all experiences that will help me grow into a loving presence of creative expression.

The world I see reflects the beauty or the horror that lives within me.

19. Look unto yourself and be saved. We are our own saviors.

God did not give me freedom of choice so that He would have to save me from myself.

God demonstrates faith in me by giving me the freedom to choose my way out of limitation whenever I make the decision.

My salvation is dependent on my ability to face what limits me.

20. Spirit can only do for us what it can do through us.

I am an embodiment of universal mind and spirit.

I am open to my indwelling spirit for guidance in my creative expression.

My creative expression is my gifts and talents manifested on the Earth.

21. Faith is a belief so great that you cannot possibly conceive of the opposite.

I am tested in my faith concerning what I believe in love and fear.

Faith in goodness and love grows as I place this faith in overcoming fearful situations.

Soon, love and compassion are all I give.

22. I am living in the Law of Grace where there is no duality, right or wrong, good or bad.

I am living in a world called heaven on Earth.

I am drawn back to this space when fear attempts to enter my doorway.

I remember from that sacred place that dwells within that there is no fear that I am unable to address.

I am whole in the presence of Love within me.

23. What we seek, seeks us.

I am divinely guided to fulfill what I came here to give.

As I awaken to my gifts, so shall I receive the beauty of my spiritual talents to give.

I am giving what Spirit has guided me to enhance the lives of others on Earth.

24. I do not "earn" Spiritual Truth. My role is to open to it.

I am given truth as I open my inner awareness to these truths.

The more I focus on Love and its truth, the more I receive.

I am the vessel through which Love can give me my most profound messages.

Our individual belief system is the foundation from which we experience our lives and through which our experiences are manifested. There are no circumstances existing that randomly come into our lives that are not supported by our belief system. Your experiences are the biggest clue to what lies within your deepest level of being through your beliefs. The outer world and the people who interact with our lives are only a reflection of what lives within.

This foundation is very important as a guide to our energies and how we use them. Awareness of these energies is helpful to those who can feel when the energy changes from love into fear. This can happen suddenly. In any interaction with another person, something that you see or hear supports the energy of Love or drops your energy in a lower space. As you become more in tune with these different vibrations of energy, your keen awareness will become more enlightened. Discernment is critical to develop when you are looking at different energies. Basically, if the energy is uplifting, enlightening, opens your heart, and you feel you are surrounded by love, then you are in the higher vibrations of Love. On the other hand, if you feel anger, jealousy, or bitterness, this energy of Love has become twisted and inverted and is supported by a false belief that is based in fear.

We have all been spiritual babies, seeking to find answers as we move through our spiritual journey. As we evolve in our spiritual growth, new insights and awarenesses develop and we become conscious that we are indeed guided in our spiritual journey. Nature becomes more involved with our lives as it continually gives clues to our spiritual nature. We interact with others differently. We begin to see a bigger picture of what our experiences give us. We interact with like-minded people that bring even greater joy to our human existence. We see clearly from spiritual eyes and hear from spiritual ears. Our journey on Earth begins to shift and change form.

The reality that appeared to be real in our past begins to transform. What does not serve us begins to die away. We release the past experiences and only take with us what we learned from each. Over time, this builds the wisdom that dwells within us. With each spiritual awakening and new revelation that elevates us to a greater understanding and knowledge of Spirit, we build the foundation for understanding that we are each an enlightened being living in a physical body.

When an experience shakes your foundation of reality, I have learned from Carla to ask questions:

- What did I learn from this experience?

- What is it trying to communicate and teach me?

- What do I need to listen to that I am not hearing or see that I am not seeing?

Life is asking you to step back for a moment to meet with your spirit and your true self to experience your insightful connection with Love. When you can respond with a higher awareness, instead of an immediate reaction of fear, you are growing into a foundation of spiritual insight that can assist you in overcoming any obstacle that may arise.

These concepts have helped to guide me on my journey through life. Whenever I am at a loss and need guidance, I reference these spiritual principles that help me comprehend what I do not understand that is fear-driven. When we have mastered fear, we will know when it presents itself off and on in our daily lives. As fear loses control over our lives and we heal our inner wounds, we can live in a place that abides in peace more frequently and consistently. That is when the Law of Grace enters our lives to allow us to experience heaven on Earth. We live in a world of possibilities and experiencing heaven on Earth has been my greatest wish from many years ago, since that time that I spoke to my Mary guide through Carla. I believed it to be possible, and believed it can happen for all of us who inhabit the Earth. The greatest gift beyond Love is to conquer our fears, experience self-love within, and know that we are temporarily living in a human body that we can elevate to heavenly heights, just as Jesus did. That is what He taught his disciples and all who lived beyond: "Truly, truly I say to you, the one who believes in Me, the works that I do, he will do also; and greater *works* than these he will do; because I am going to the Father." *New American Standard Bible*, John 14:12.

Jesus believed in us to find our way, and that was his gift to us. We are given the way with our spiritual hearts open to Love. We no longer have to dwell in fear unless that is our choice. Our life and how we live it belongs to us. Choose wisely: Love or fear.

Healing Love Practice

The Awareness:

Our guiding light is the indwelling Love that directs our path.

What new awareness brings insights to a brighter future?

What stands out for you to implement in your life now?

My Affirmation

I have the awareness of indwelling
Love that assists me to new heights.

SUGGESTED READING

Barker, Raymond Charles. *The Power of Decision* (Revised and Updated Edition). © 1968, 1988 by Raymond Charles Barker, Publisher, Dodd, Mead & Company. © 2011 by Richard Collins, Published by Tarcher-Perigee, an imprint of Penguin RandomHouse, LLC

> Note: I own the published edition from 1988, the Revised and Updated Edition. The 2011 edition is now available on Amazon books for $17. The 1968 edition is pretty expensive for a book: used $38 or new $75.

Cohen, Alan. *A Course in Miracles, Made Easy,* © 2015 by Alan Cohen, and *Spirit Means Business,* © 2019 by Alan Cohen. Published by Hay House, Inc.

> Note: I read the original *A Course in Miracles* © 1975 by the Foundation for Inner Peace in the mid 1980s. It took me a year to read and absorb what was being taught. This was a difficult read and is probably the reason Alan masterfully created an easier version to comprehend and make useful for us to implement in our daily lives.

Fox, Emmet. *Power Through Constructive Thinking.* © 1932-1940 by Emmet Fox, © Renewed 1968 by Kathleen Whelan; Harper & Row, Publishers, Inc.

Harris, Lee. *Conversations with the Z's, Book One: The Energetics of the New Human Soul.* © 2022 by Lee Harris, and *Conversations with the Z's, Book Two: Awaken Your Multidimensional Soul.* © 2023 by Lee Harris; Publisher, Lee Harris Energy, LLC

Holmes, Ernest. *The Science of Mind: The Complete Original 1926 Edition.* © 1926 by Ernest Holmes and © 2022 First St. Martin's Essentials Edition, Published by St Martin's Publishing Group

Moorjani, Anita. *Dying To Be Me, My Journey from Cancer, to Near Death, to True Healing.* © 2012 by Anita Moorjani, Published by Hay House, Inc.

Shanti Christo Foundation. Three volume set, *The Way of Mastery: The Way of the Heart, The Way of Transformation, The Way of Knowing.* © by Shanti Christo Foundation www.shantichristo.com.

Singer, Michael A. *Living Untethered, Beyond the Human Predicament.* © 2022 by Michael Singer, and *The Untethered Soul, The Journey Beyond Yourself.* © 2007 by Michael Singer; New Harbinger Publications

> Note: I found *Living Untethered* a much easier read, and it may be that reading *The Untethered Soul* first is the reason.

Tolle, Eckhart. *The Power of Now, A Guide to Spiritual Enlightenment.* © 1999 by Eckhart Tolle; Namaste Publishing in Canada and then New World Library in the U.S.

ACKNOWLEDGEMENTS

I have so much gratitude for the people who have helped me on my journey to bring this book to life. The road is not always easy, but when you have love and support on the journey it lightens the load. I felt alone in the beginning of my writing. One prayer to God when I knew I could not do this alone brought a multitude of talented and skillful people into my life to give me the support to complete what I had started. I want to thank you all for being my support as an author and a contributor to a life worth living:

Kelly Fisher, thank you for your mediumship that delivered the message to write my book. My spiritual council came through strong and clear, and the name of the book never wavered. You are very gifted with your talents of delivering divine messages and I am grateful.

Alan Cohen, thank you for inspiring me to be a higher version of me. You elevated me as the baton was passed from Carla to you. I am grateful for your work and you guiding me forward with my life. You facilitated bringing some amazing journeys through spirit.

Carla Gordan, thank you for bringing spiritual awareness into my life. My journey in life would have so many missing links without your teachings and the love you gave to all your students. I am grateful that spirit guided me to you, as my life has been forever blessed. Even though you are in the spirit world now, I know you have already received this message.

Tony Robbins, you came into my life in the 1990s. I was guided to you for a reason. You taught me to never give up, to believe in myself, and how to go beyond boundaries. I was blessed by Mastery University, Leadership Academy, Leadership Date with Destiny, and more.

Michael Singer, you have been a great teacher through all of your books I have read that deeply impacted my life.

Lee Harris and the Zs, I have so much appreciation with discovering and following you while writing my book. You were my big inspiration for sharpening my connection with the spiritual world and channeled writing. Spirit has always been my inspiration.

Steve Harrison, thank you and your brother for creating Bradley Communications. I have been so enriched by all the personal growth and development from the programs you offer.

Jack Canfield, I appreciate the knowledge and inspiration of your wisdom from the Jack Canfield / Steve Harrison Mastermind Retreat I attended in 2022 and 2023. I learned so much as a new author and where to take my work beyond my book.

Geoffrey Berwind, thank you for your talent and expertise in storytelling and speaking. My self-development as an author and speaker has grown with your contribution and help.

Cristina Smith, thank you for coaching me through the journey with my book. You have always been on target with seeing me to the end. I am grateful to have you as a supportive coach to answer any needs or questions and for wisdom and knowledge of the book industry.

Valerie Costa, my editor, you are a master of adding the shining touches to enhance my manuscript. I am so grateful for your expertise as an editor.

Christy Day, thank you for my gorgeous book cover and interior design of this book. I appreciate your patience in working with me to bring the cover design toward its finishing touches. I appreciate your talent.

Kris Carlson and Debra Evans, thank you for your support with your classes I attended with Book Doulas and the Momentum class. This was a great start for a first-time author, and I value what I learned from both of you. Debra, thank you for the idea of adding a "Healing Love Practice." I am grateful for your support and inspiration.

My First Readers, thank you for your time to go on this journey with me. Your input has been invaluable to the book. I entrusted you to give me honest feedback, and you delivered in a genuine, constructive way. I am deeply grateful to you.

The Divine Nine, you know who you are. I am so appreciative of having a soul connection with my tribe of spiritual friends and the bond of support we give each other whenever needed. We met as strangers and became family, with our strong heart connections.

To my family, you have given so much encouragement in supporting my efforts in writing this book. I always love how you believe in me. I am truly grateful for your love and support.

ABOUT THE AUTHOR

LINDA F. KENT is a new author who has experienced the ups and downs of life, found the spiritual world, and implemented the lessons, knowledge, and wisdom she has learned in her spiritual journey into her life. She believes that we all have insight and the ability to change our lives by using the love within to heal anything that would hold us back from our true gifts of spirit that live within each of us.

Linda has been a successful physical therapist for thirty-five years, using her training and her spiritual insight to help the patients she has served. She is a holistic life coach and uses her intuitive guidance during her sessions to give greater depth and clarity to her clients.

Her mission in her new career as an author, teacher, and speaker is to awaken a new presence in the world. Linda loves how spirit always moves her into new adventures in her life. She believes that life is exciting and elevating if you allow it to be.

Linda Kent is available for speaking engagements,
media interviews and other services.

Visit her website at: www.lindafkent.com
or email her here: linda@lindafkent.com

Made in the USA
Coppell, TX
26 January 2024